Decades of American History

AMERICA IN THE 1960s

JIM CALLAN

Facts On File, Inc.

A Stonesong Press Book
Decades of American History: *America in the 1960s*

Copyright © 2006 by Stonesong Press, LLC

Facts On File, Inc.
132 West 31st Street
New York NY 10001

Library of Congress Cataloging-in-Publication Data

Callan, Jim.
  America in the 1960s / Jim Callan.
     p. cm.—(Decades of American history)
  "A Stonesong Press book."
  Includes bibliographical references and index.
  ISBN 0-8160-5642-0
1. United States—History—1961–1969—Juvenile literature. 2. Nineteen
sixties—Juvenile literature. I. Title. II. Series.
  E841.C27 2005
  973.922—dc22

                                                    2005011876

Facts On File books are available at special discounts when purchased in bulk quantities
for businesses, associations, institutions, or sales promotions. Please call our Special Sales
Department in New York at (212) 967-8800 or (800) 322-8755.

You can find Facts On File on the World Wide Web at http://www.factsonfile.com

Text design by Laura Smyth, Smythetype
Photo research by Larry Schwartz
Cover design by Perhsson Design

Printed in the United States of America

VB PKG 10 9 8 7 6 5 4 3 2 1

This book is printed on acid-free paper.

CONTENTS

CHAPTER 1

THE UNITED STATES IN 1960

AS 1960 BEGAN, THE SEEDS FOR CHANGE in the United States were already evident. It was an election year and Dwight D. Eisenhower, the outgoing president, was the oldest commander-in-chief in the history of the nation. In the 1960 election, he was replaced by the youngest president ever elected to the office, Senator John F. Kennedy. Kennedy was the first president born in the 20th century, and he was also the first to use television to influence an election. His strong showing during the televised presidential debates against opponent Vice-President Richard Nixon helped him to win the election.

In November 1960, Americans elected John F. Kennedy to the presidency. *(Library of Congress)*

Kennedy's victory was just one indication of the growing emphasis on youth in U.S. culture. The youth movement, which had started in the 1950s with rock 'n' roll and the Beat Generation, continued to grow. In 1960, young people were reading Beat writer Jack Kerouac's novel *On the Road*, which rejected mainstream U.S. society. They also welcomed back their rock 'n' roll idol, Elvis Presley, from his two-year stint in the army.

As during the 1950s, Americans continued to enjoy a prosperous economy. In 1960, many families had two cars and lived in the suburbs, where they shopped at the new convenient shopping malls. Television was still the main form of entertainment, and over 90 percent of U.S. homes owned at least one television set. New television shows in 1960 included *The Flintstones, The Andy Griffith Show,* and *My Three Sons,* continuing the dominance of light family comedies. Some of the popular movies of 1960, however, took a darker look at the United States. *Psycho* was a horrifying tale of a psychotic murderer, *The Apartment* was a cynical look at the morals of the business world, and *On the Beach* depicted the end of the world after a nuclear war.

Average family income in 1960 was only $5,600, but many products were much less expensive than they are today. For example, a cheeseburger cost about 20 cents, with fries an extra 10 cents. Candy bars were only 5 cents, and milk was 25 cents a quart. A Volkswagen Beetle was the second car for many families and cost only $1,675. Men could buy a seersucker suit for $20, and a woman's full-length bridal gown could be had for $36.50.

In 1960, African Americans in the United States still had little power. There were no black senators and only four black men in the House of Representatives, but the civil rights movement was prominent enough in 1960 that presidential candidate Kennedy offered his help to the wife of black leader Martin Luther King Jr. when he was in jail.

Women also had little power in 1960. There were only 20 women members of Congress, and only 35

> *"Like an eating cancer, segregation destroys the morale of our citizens and disfigures our country throughout the world."*
>
> —NAACP leader Thurgood Marshall, who later became a Supreme Court Justice

percent of women worked in 1960. In May, the birth control pill, which prevents pregnancy, became available to women. In 1960, "the pill" sparked a debate among Americans about the role of women in U.S. society. In the decade of the 1960s, this debate ignited a powerful women's movement.

THE CALM BEFORE THE STORM

The 1960s are known as a decade of upheaval. What made the 1960s so turbulent? The forces of change started during the previous decade, in the post–World War II years of the 1950s. During periods of postwar recovery, such as after World War II in the late 1940s and 1950s, and after World War I in the 1920s, many Americans felt the need to recover, to ignore the problems of the world, and to enjoy life. After World War I came the Roaring Twenties, a decade of automobiles, speakeasies, jazz, and prosperity. Post–World War II United States was a time of televisions, the baby boom, suburban homes, and a thriving economy. But the issues that made the United States explode in the 1960s had their roots in the 1950s.

World War II hero Dwight D. Eisenhower was president for most of the 1950s. Affectionately called Ike by the public, Eisenhower was not an activist. He thought the president should stay out of political and social battles. He preferred to suggest policies and let Congress make the final decisions. As a result, some critics called him "the standstill president," but his approach suited the mood of the country, and he was immensely popular throughout his two terms.

Eisenhower's main issue was world peace. As commander of the Allied forces in World War II, he had seen the brutality and waste of war and believed he should

"Every gun that is made, every warship launched is a theft from those who hunger and are not fed, from those who are cold and are not clothed."

—President Eisenhower on the waste of military costs

American paratroopers receive their D-day orders from General Eisenhower. Before he became president in the 1950s, Eisenhower commanded the Allied troops in World War II. *(Library of Congress)*

Joseph Stalin was the all-powerful leader of the Soviet Union. Although he died in 1953, the cold war his policies created loomed over U.S.-Soviet relations throughout the 1960s. *(Library of Congress)*

"We must have compassion and understanding for those who hate us. So many people have been taught to hate, taught from the cradle. They are not totally responsible."

—Martin Luther King Jr., explaining his views on nonviolent protest during the Montgomery bus boycott

use the power of the presidency to promote peace. He was particularly concerned about the cold war, the high state of tension that had developed between the United States and the Soviet Union. Eisenhower had some successes during his first term. He played a key role in securing a cease-fire between the warring nations of North Korea and South Korea, and he advanced his "atoms for peace" plan at the United Nations. Under the plan, U.S. scientists were permitted to share their knowledge of atomic power with other nations so that they could use nuclear power for peaceful purposes. At a 1955 conference in Geneva, Switzerland, Eisenhower assured the Soviet Union that the United States would never take part in an aggressive war against them. The Soviet Union and the United States also agreed to an extensive cultural exchange program. The cold war seemed to thaw for a couple of years.

Eisenhower's second term presented many more problems. The U.S. economy weakened, the Soviet Union enjoyed success in space exploration with its Sputnik program, and the aging president struggled with health problems, including a moderately serious heart attack. In 1956, a war broke out in the Middle East when Egypt seized the Suez Canal from British and French control. British and French troops regained the canal, and the Soviet Union threatened to enter the conflict until diplomacy eventually settled the crisis. The canal was returned to Egypt, but the cold war was back in the headlines. In 1957, Eisenhower made enemies at home with his position on civil rights, when he sent federal troops to Little Rock, Arkansas, to enforce the Supreme Court ruling on the desegregation of public schools.

CIVIL RIGHTS

Race relations in the Americas had been a big problem from the time African slaves were introduced to the North American and Caribbean colonies in the 1600s,

and they remained a serious issue throughout U.S. history. After the Civil War and the defeat of the slave-holding southern states, southern whites rejected free African Americans, which led to two separate societies in the South, one white and one black. As southern society recovered, blacks were excluded. In 1896, the Supreme Court upheld segregation with its *Plessy v. Ferguson* "separate but equal" ruling, but conditions in the South were not equal among whites and blacks. Most African Americans lived in poverty and were deprived of education and many civil rights, including voting and education. The Ku Klux Klan and other white supremacist groups, who believed in the superiority of the white race, terrorized African Americans with beatings and lynchings to maintain segregation. By the beginning of the 20th century, black leaders had emerged to fight for blacks' civil rights, but it was not until the middle of the 20th century that U.S. society really began to change.

African-American students often had to endure the insults and threats of white students to attend their new schools in the South. *(Library of Congress)*

THE STRUGGLE GROWS

An important event in the civil rights movement occurred on May 17, 1954, when the Supreme Court ruled on the historic case, *Brown v. Board of Education of Topeka, Kansas*. The Court ruled that school segregation laws were unconstitutional and ordered 17 states with such laws to integrate their schools immediately. The legal victory proved to be mainly symbolic for a number of years because many state, county, and city governments in the South passed laws to avoid school integration.

Another milestone in the civil rights movement occurred on December 1, 1955, in Montgomery, Alabama. An African-American woman, Rosa Parks, refused to give up her seat on a bus to a white man as a city law required, and she was arrested. The local National Association for the Advancement of Colored People (NAACP) organized a boycott of city buses by blacks to protest the discrimination. A local black minister, Martin Luther King Jr. became one of the leaders of the protest, preaching a message of nonviolence. More than a year later, on December 20, 1956, the Supreme Court struck down the Montgomery bus laws as unconstitutional.

In summer 1957, a federal court ordered the all-white Central High School in Little Rock, Arkansas, to admit nine African-American students. On the first day of school, September 5, 1957, the students were denied entrance when Governor Orval Faubus ordered the Arkansas National Guard to surround the building. White mobs also gathered outside the school to protest and threaten violence. President Eisenhower met with Governor Faubus and ordered him to admit the black students, but Faubus still refused.

On September 23, police escorted the students into the school although the white crowds outside the school

A Little Rock, Arkansas, high school student watches her teacher on a special broadcast. In 1958, Little Rock officials closed the schools to avoid integration, necessitating the broadcasts. *(Library of Congress)*

THE SPACE RACE

The cold war space race between the United States and the Soviet Union began on October 4, 1957, when the Soviet Union launched *Sputnik 1,* the first human-made satellite, into orbit around the earth. The object only contained a radio transmitter, a battery, and some aerials, but to the U.S. government, it meant the Soviet Union could launch bombs in the same way and drop them on the United States. One month later, the Soviet Union launched the larger *Sputnik 2,* which carried the world's first space traveler, a dog named Laika. Laika died after one week when her oxygen ran out, but the mission proved that living things could survive in space.

The United States tried to catch up to the Soviets in December 1957 when it launched its first satellite, but it blew up on the launchpad. The press quickly called the failure "Flopnik" and "Kaputnik." The United States had its first success one month later, however, with the launch of *Explorer 1*. This satellite carried a Geiger counter on board that detected layers of radiation above the Earth's atmosphere. These layers later became known as the Van Allen belts.

The Soviet Union quickly showed that it had a superior command of space technology with *Sputnik 3* in May 1958 and the lunar probes, *Lunik 1* and *2* in 1959. *Sputnik 3* weighed over a ton and carried the first space laboratory, which transmitted information about the upper atmosphere back to Earth. *Lunik 1* was the first satellite to leave Earth's orbit, and *Lunik 2* made a planned crash landing on the moon's surface two days after launch.

Somewhat lost in the attention given to the space race were two U.S. inventions in 1958 that later proved as important as any space voyage. The first was the invention of the integrated circuit, the forerunner of the computer microchip. The integrated circuit was first assembled by engineer Jack Kilby and would later become vital for smaller and faster computers. The other was the development of lasers, powerful beams of light that were used later in hundreds of ways in communication, medicine, the military, and industry.

The United States entered the space race with *Explorer 1* in 1958. The satellite reached an altitude of 1,600 miles above Earth during its mission. *(NASA)*

---

rioted and attacked the white reporters covering the event. That night, Eisenhower ordered federal troops to Little Rock to restore order. Each black student was given a bodyguard for protection. The victory once again proved short-lived, as Governor Faubus shut down the entire city school system the following year. Many white students enrolled in private schools that did not have to be integrated. However, the incident showed that the federal government was willing to try to enforce civil rights laws. It would try even harder in the 1960s.

J. Edgar Hoover served under eight presidents as leader of the FBI. He feared communism and contributed to the Red Scare policies of the 1950s. *(Library of Congress)*

"The war after that will be fought with stones."

—Scientist Albert Einstein, when asked his opinion of the outcome of nuclear war

THE COLD WAR

After World War II, most Americans hoped to enjoy a period of peace and security. However, one of the United States's former wartime allies quickly turned into a formidable foe. The Soviet Union's communist leader, Joseph Stalin, immediately declared the United States to be its enemy. He set up and supported communist governments in Poland, East Germany, and Hungary, and he made sure the Soviet Union developed nuclear bombs to equal those of the United States. A new kind of conflict was developing, known as the cold war.

The cold war conflict pitted two very different economic and political systems against each other—the capitalist democracies of the United States and Western Europe versus the communist dictatorships of the Soviet Union and the People's Republic of China. Each side feared that the other's goal was world conquest, so each tried to pressure other nations to become its allies. (A capitalist democracy includes private ownership and control of property as well as a government of elected representatives; Soviet and Chinese communism involves the government's control of society, particularly the production and distribution of wealth and goods, usually under the rule of a dictator.)

Because both the United States and the Soviet Union had nuclear weapons, each knew that military conflict could lead to the destruction of most of the world in a nuclear war, so the cold war was usually waged in other ways. Yet nuclear weapons were stockpiled in staggering numbers during the 1950s as each superpower tried to maintain a nuclear superiority to deter the other from launching a military attack. There was a constant war of words as each side condemned the other. Smaller nations were persuaded with economic and military aid to ally with one side or the other.

The cold war spread to the home front as Americans began to fear communists within the country. Called the Red Scare, fear led to hysteria as the communist label was attached to anyone who criticized U.S. society, including civil rights leaders, union organizers, college teachers, and artists. A few communist spies did work inside the United States, and they gave atomic secrets to the Soviets, enabling them to develop nuclear weapons more quickly.

The Red Scare reached its peak during the Senate investigations conducted by Senator Joseph McCarthy of Wisconsin. McCarthy claimed he had the names of Communist Party members within the State Department. What he actually had were the names of some Americans who were interested in communism during the 1930s, and who were in support of the labor movement, though they had since totally renounced communism. McCarthy had obtained many of these names from another staunch anticommunist, J. Edgar Hoover, director of the Federal Bureau of Investigation (FBI).

As McCarthy realized he had no proof of his accusations, he resorted to lies and gossip and spread his investigation to Hollywood movie actors and directors. He never presented any proof, but the hysteria of the time resulted in a Hollywood blacklist of writers and directors who were forbidden to work in the industry. In addition, more than 600 college professors were fired because of his false accusations. A Senate committee eventually censured McCarthy formally, ending his reign of terror, but a fear of communism remained strong in the United States. The cold war escalated in the 1960s, bringing the world to the brink of nuclear war and to another war in Asia.

VIETNAM

Since the end of World War II, France had been trying to put down a communist revolt in its colony of French Indochina in Southeast Asia. The rebels, called the Viet Minh, were led by Vietnamese leader Ho Chi Minh. They demanded independence for Vietnam. By 1950, as

"Until this moment, Senator, I think I never really gauged your cruelty or your recklessness. Have you left no sense of decency?"

—U.S. Army lawyer Joseph Welch, attacking Senator McCarthy's methods during his anticommunist hearings

"I will not cut my conscience to fit this year's fashion."

—Writer Lillian Hellman, on her refusal to testify about anyone other than herself at Senator Joseph McCarthy's anticommunist hearings

On July 8, 1959, Major Dale Buis and Sergeant Chester Ovnand became the first U.S. soldiers killed in Vietnam. They fell during a communist guerilla raid on the U.S. military base at Bien Hoa.

France was losing the war, it asked for aid from the United States. Anxious to stop the spread of communism, President Harry Truman approved the aid. By 1954, the United States was paying 80 percent of France's war costs.

In May 1954, French troops surrendered to Viet Minh forces at Dien Bien Phu in Vietnam, ending the French occupation. France had asked President Eisenhower if U.S. troops would intervene, but he refused. At a peace conference in Geneva, Switzerland, two months later, the French and the Viet Minh agreed to temporarily divide Vietnam into two sections until reunification elections could take place in 1956. The United States became concerned because Ho Chi Minh and the Viet Minh had become communist. Until the elections, the communists ruled North Vietnam, and a noncommunist leader, Ngo Dinh Diem, ruled South Vietnam, at the United States's insistence.

Two years later, however, Diem refused to hold elections because it was clear that Ho Chi Minh would win and unify the country under the communist flag. Eisenhower assured Diem that the United States would support South Vietnam with as much financial aid as it needed to stay noncommunist. Eisenhower also sent military advisers to South Vietnam to create and train its army. Diem proved to be an oppressive dictator, and a rebel movement within South Vietnam called the National Liberation Front (NLF), also known as the Viet Cong, joined the North Vietnamese in seeking Diem's overthrow. In response, one of Eisenhower's last acts as president in December 1960 was to increase the number of U.S. troops (still called advisers) in South Vietnam to around 1,000.

SOCIAL TRENDS

Americans of the 1950s tried very hard to prevent international problems from spoiling the good lives many found in the prosperity of the decade. Military

Levitt & Sons construction firm built three entire towns called Levittown, helping create the suburban lifestyle of the 1960s. The one pictured is in Pennsylvania. *(National Archives)*

production escalated, fueled by the demands of the cold war, and much new technology was developed. These events made the economy strong. Since World War II, many veterans took advantage of the benefits of the G.I. Bill. The bill provided veterans (former G.I.s) with an affordable college education and low-interest home loans. The college education resulted in better jobs. In addition, powerful unions secured better wages for workers.

The boom in the construction of new homes led to the development of the suburbs. Thousands of inexpensive homes were built outside of large cities throughout the country. The homes were often identical to each other, but with prices as low as $8,000, veterans and other young people, who were starting their careers and families, jumped at the chance to own their first home.

The optimism of the decade also led to the baby boom. Between 1946 and 1964, 30 million babies were born. The peak of the boom was in the late 1950s, when more than 4 million births occurred each year. One result of the baby boom and the strong economy was a huge prosperous middle class with spending power. The other result was a change in the role of women. Because one salary could support a family, most mothers stayed at home to care for the children. Those

The Eisenhowers watch Ike get the 1952 Republican presidential nomination. Television became a main source of news for Americans in the 1950s. *(Library of Congress)*

women who worked outside the home were usually employed in low-paying jobs and worked as secretaries, nurses, and teachers.

The decade was marked by conformity. Millions of families shared the same postwar experiences and had similar jobs and incomes, homes, and families. After the hard times of the depression and World War II, many Americans embraced the security that came with being much like their neighbors. Many people avoided being different or speaking out on social issues because this behavior could make one an object of suspicion, or even earn one the label of communist. In spite of this situation, there was dissent and independent thought nevertheless.

ROCK 'N' ROLL AND BEATNIKS

Nonconformity was most obvious in two major cultural developments: rock 'n' roll music and the Beat movement. Teens, who had started to develop their own

Long hair was not immediately popular in the 1960s. In 1960, most men wore crew cuts while women maintained elaborate bouffant hairstyles.

MOVIES REFLECT TEENAGE REBELLION

In 1950, sociologist David Riesman wrote *The Lonely Crowd,* a book about the pressures of conformity in U.S. society. Riesman said that even if conformity brings wealth, it forces people to live according to a rigid set of social standards rather than their own personal standards. As a result, many people lose their sense of identity and feel lonely and confused. This description was particularly true of teens in the1950s, and it led to strong feelings of rebellion among many of them.

J. D. Salinger's 1951 novel *The Catcher in the Rye* deals with the theme of teenage alienation, but it was not until the mid-1950s that Hollywood realized teens were changing. In 1954, the movie *The Wild One* starred actor Marlon Brando as the leader of a motorcycle gang that terrorizes a small town. Brando's young character is moody and confused. When asked by one of the locals, "What are you rebelling against?" Brando replied, "Whaddya got?" This question echoed the restless feelings of many teens.

In 1955, the movie *Blackboard Jungle* appeared. It deals with the problem of juvenile delinquency in schools. Glenn Ford plays a teacher who has to contend with students whose feelings of not belonging turn violent. The scene in which a student pulls a knife on a teacher shocked many adults and led to riots in some theaters. The response of audiences revealed that teen alienation was becoming a social issue in U.S. society. The movie's theme song, "Rock Around the Clock," became the first rock 'n' roll song to reach the top of the charts.

That same year, *Rebel Without a Cause,* a movie starring James Dean, presented a more personal look at teen suffering. Dean's character realizes that his rebellion is a symptom of a larger problem—of young people's need to find a way to be understood and accepted in a society run by adults. Dean was already a teen idol when the film was released, but he would not enjoy its success. He was killed in a car crash a month before it appeared in movie theaters.

culture in the 1930s, expressed their independence in the 1950s through rock 'n' roll. The music had its roots in 1951 in Cleveland, Ohio, when radio disc jockey Alan Freed started to play African-American rhythm and blues songs. This music was a variation of blues, which had been around since the early part of the 20th century. Freed started calling the music rock 'n' roll, based on the title of one of the songs, and his show was an instant success. In 1953, the white group Bill Haley and his Comets had a hit song in which they added some elements of country music to the rhythm and blues sound, and rock 'n' roll was born. In 1955, Haley's "Rock Around the Clock" sold more than 1 million copies.

It was not until 1956 that the music found its first white superstar and became the sound of a generation. Elvis Presley became the idol of millions of young people with his good looks and soulful voice. Starting with "Heartbreak Hotel" in 1956, Presley stayed at the top of

"If I thought that was true, I would go back to driving a truck."

—Rock 'n' roll star Elvis Presley, when asked if he thought his songs contributed to juvenile delinquency in the United States

Beat writer Jack Kerouac published four books in 1960: *Tristessa, Visions of Cody, The Scripture of the Golden Eternity,* and *Lonesome Traveler,* all adding to his influence on the counterculture of the decade to follow.

One of the greatest medical breakthroughs of the century occurred in 1954 when Dr. Jonas Salk developed a polio vaccine. By the mid-1960s, the disease had virtually disappeared in the United States.

Billboard magazine's bestselling record list for 55 weeks. His other hits during that time were "Hound Dog," "Don't Be Cruel," "All Shook Up," "Love Me Tender," and "Jailhouse Rock," all selling well over 1 million copies each. When Presley entered military service in 1958, rock 'n' roll went into a minor decline. The 1960s would see it come back bigger than ever.

Beatniks were part of the counterculture of the 1950s. The name was derived from a group of writers called the Beat Generation or the Beats, which included Jack Kerouac, Allen Ginsberg, and Lawrence Ferlinghetti. Kerouac first used the word *beat* to mean that the individual had been beaten down by the mass conformity of postwar U.S. society. He later connected the term to *beatific,* or blessed, and many other writers expressed their understanding of the term. Many followers of the new culture, called beatniks, rejected the materialism of U.S. society, the dullness of suburban culture, and the cold war conflict.

Beat writers and their beatnik followers embraced jazz music, drugs, casual sex, and anything else that was unconventional to assert their individuality. After Kerouac wrote the most popular Beat novel, *On the Road* (1957) about his adventures and discoveries on a cross-country trip, many beatniks set out on similar journeys. The excitement of an alternative lifestyle appealed to many teens and college students who were searching for an answer to their fears and confusions about the world's problems. Beatniks began a counterculture that would grow much larger in the 1960s.

TELEVISION

Along with the automobile and the computer, television had the greatest influence on Americans of all the inventions of the 20th century. It did not simply provide entertainment, it also changed Americans' lifestyles and their view of the world. In 1950, a little over 4 million

Ticket lines at movie theaters grew shorter as Americans stayed home to watch television. *(Library of Congress)*

Americans had a television set; by 1960, the number was 50 million and growing. The first effect of this development was that people stayed home more often, causing many entertainment businesses to suffer. In the early 1950s, movie attendance dropped 40 percent and many theaters closed down. Radio survived by becoming a source of music and news. Book sales also dropped.

At first, television programming was varied and included children's shows, documentaries, staged dramas, variety shows, adventures, and arts and culture programming shows such as opera. Comedies (also known as situation comedies or sitcoms) were very popular and included Milton Berle's *Texaco Star Theater* and *I Love Lucy*. As television's popularity grew, program sponsors realized they could reach huge audiences with their advertising. After seeing an effective television ad, millions of Americans might buy the same product. By 1952, sponsors were already spending $128 million on these ads and the three main television networks—

Milton Berle's television show was so popular, it once had a 94.7 rating. This statistic meant that more than 94 percent of all the television sets that were turned on were tuned to his show.

Two states were added to the country in 1959— Alaska on January 3 and Hawaii on August 21. They were the 49th and 50th states to be added.

CBS, NBC, and ABC—were showing huge profits. With large sums of money involved, the sponsors insisted that the networks provide a more limited range of programming, including only those shows that would appeal to a mass audience. By the late 1950s, television was dominated by family comedies, westerns, and quiz shows. Conformity was good for business and television had become a tool of business.

There were no shows featuring minorities at the end of the decade, and shows addressing social issues were almost nonexistent, but that would start to change with the development of television news shows. As popular as television was in the 1950s, it was not until the nightly news broadcasts of the 1960s, which broadcast national and world events, that television achieved its greatest influence.

CHAPTER 2

THE ARRIVAL OF CAMELOT, 1960–1961

THE PROBLEMS OF PRESIDENT EISEN-hower's second term made many Americans question his leadership. In 1960, the final year of his presidency, Eisenhower tried to reestablish his standing and leave office on a positive note by taking a world tour promoting peace. Starting in December 1959, Eisenhower visited 11 countries from Spain to India. In February 1960, he went on a goodwill tour of Latin America. He was also scheduled to visit the Soviet Union in May for an important summit conference with the Soviet premier, Nikita Khrushchev.

President Kennedy meets with Russian leader Nikita Khrushchev in 1961. At the time, Khrushchev was secretly planning to send nuclear weapons to Cuba. *(National Park Service)*

President Eisenhower was 70 years old when he left office in 1961. The 1960s started with the youngest president ever elected—President Kennedy was 43. *(Library of Congress)*

"I'm convinced that no military victory is possible."

—President Eisenhower, speaking about the growing conflict in Vietnam, 1957

On May 1, 1960, this plan changed when a U.S. U-2 spy plane was shot down over the Soviet Union. Eisenhower had approved surveillance flights to keep track of military developments inside the Soviet Union. At first, the U.S. government claimed that the plane was on a weather-tracking mission and had accidentally strayed off course. The truth was revealed when the Soviet Union announced that the U-2 pilot, Francis Gary Powers, was alive and had admitted he was on a spy mission.

Khrushchev demanded an end to the flights over the Soviet Union and an apology from Eisenhower. The president agreed to stop the flights but would not apologize. Khrushchev canceled the upcoming conference with Eisenhower and accused the United States of treachery and aggression. Powers was put on trial in Moscow and sentenced to 10 years in a Soviet prison. (He would only serve two years, until an exchange of spies was arranged between the two governments.)

Eisenhower's effectiveness as a world leader was over. Japan canceled a scheduled visit by the president, due to an outbreak of anti-U.S. riots. At a session of the United Nations General Assembly in September, Khrushchev and Fidel Castro, the communist leader of Cuba, dominated the meeting with speeches condemning the United Nations and the United States. At one point, Khrushchev banged his shoe on the table to indicate his disdain for the proceedings.

To Americans watching the event on television, it seemed that the United States had lost its influence and respect. A feeling of dissatisfaction turned into a national debate about the country's purpose and goals. One political reporter attacked Eisenhower for "promoting private prosperity at the expense of national power." As the 1960s began, some Americans wondered what effect their desire for security and conformity had had on the national character. Most agreed the United States was in need of new leadership.

CIVIL RIGHTS: SIT-INS

In 1957, one year after the successful Montgomery bus boycott, Martin Luther King Jr. formed the Southern Christian Leadership Conference (SCLC). This organization of African-American churches and clergy aimed to end racial segregation in the United States. King believed the National Association for the Advancement of Colored People (NAACP) had made important legal efforts to end segregation, but he felt more direct action was also necessary.

King believed strongly in nonviolence and civil disobedience to protest the unjust laws of segregation. He advocated boycotts, demonstrations, marches, and other nonviolent protests, but he also believed the only way for protesters to earn the support of white Americans was to remain nonviolent even when physically attacked. It was no coincidence that the civil rights movement gained momentum with the rise of television. King knew that nonviolent demonstrators would probably be met with violence wherever they protested, and that television would reveal the true nature of segregation to millions of Americans. He was confident that when Americans saw violent white racists and peaceful black demonstrators, the public would come to support the civil rights movement.

The first form of civil disobedience of the 1960s was the sit-in. On February 1, 1960, four African-American college students entered a segregated Woolworth's lunch counter in Greensboro, North Carolina, and asked for a cup of coffee. No one served them and they sat peacefully at the counter until it closed. The next day, 20 African-American students protested by participating in the first sit-in. After their protest made news, sit-ins spread throughout the South. In the next two months, there were sit-ins in 54 cities in nine states.

As the sit-in movement spread, some demonstrators were thrown in jail. They would often refuse to accept bail, so that local jails became full and could not

Dr. Martin Luther King Jr.'s commitment to nonviolence helped convince many white Americans to support the civil rights movement of the 1960s. *(Library of Congress)*

"There is more power in socially organized masses on the march than there is in guns in the hands of a few desperate men."

—Martin Luther King Jr. on the power of nonviolent activism

Although President Kennedy was the youngest man ever elected president, he had served 14 years in Congress before entering the White House. *(Library of Congress)*

In 1961, the manufacturer Proctor and Gamble released the first disposable diaper, Pampers, saving millions of parents from the chore of washing and reusing cloth diapers.

"I can assure you that you will observe a vast wasteland."

—Federal Communications Commission chairman Newton Minow on the quality of television shows in 1961

hold the large numbers of protestors. In some cities, angry whites confronted the demonstrators with violence as local law enforcement stood by and did nothing. Television cameras caught the violence on film for the nightly news programs. The sit-ins were successful, and many southern cities, including Greensboro, soon integrated their lunch counters.

KENNEDY'S BACKGROUND: WEALTH AND PRIVILEGE

John Fitzgerald Kennedy was born on May 29, 1917, in Brookline, Massachusetts, a suburb next to Boston. His large family enjoyed considerable wealth and political experience. His grandfather John "Honey Fitz" Fitzgerald had been mayor of Boston, and his father, Joseph P. Kennedy, had been ambassador to Britain in 1937–1940, immediately before and just after the outbreak of World War II.

The young Kennedy was in and out of private schools due to various health problems, but he graduated cum laude (with honors) from Harvard College in 1940. His undergraduate thesis, *Why England Slept,* a study of England's appeasement of Nazi Germany before World War II, was published as a notable book. After the United States entered World War II, Kennedy joined the navy in 1941 and was made a commander of a PT (patrol torpedo) boat in the South Pacific in 1943.

Later that year, a Japanese destroyer sank Kennedy's boat, killing two crewmembers. Kennedy and the other survivors swam three miles to a nearby island, with Kennedy pulling one of his wounded men to safety the entire distance. Kennedy swam the surrounding waters for the next several days until he was able to get word to a U.S. rescue ship, and the crew was saved. He was awarded the Purple Heart medal for his courage and was sent back to the United States for medical care.

In 1944, Kennedy's older brother Joe was killed in action in the war. Joe had been prepared by their father for a career in politics. After Joe's death, Joseph Sr. pressured John to enter politics instead. John ran for a seat in the House of Representatives in 1946. He was elected and served three terms from 1946 to 1952, representing a section of Boston. In the House, Kennedy usually voted the Democratic Party line, but he criticized Democratic president Truman for not supporting Chinese Nationalists strongly enough in their struggle against the Chinese communists.

In 1952, Kennedy ran for a seat in the U.S. Senate against the popular Republican incumbent Henry Cabot Lodge Jr. Kennedy won, even though Republican President Eisenhower easily won the state's electoral votes. Kennedy's victory made national politicians notice him as one of the Democrats' rising stars. Kennedy's first term as senator was hindered by two serious back operations and a long recovery. During the recuperation, he wrote *Profiles in Courage,* a book about U.S. leaders who risked their careers by fighting for unpopular but just causes. The book later won a Pulitzer Prize.

Kennedy made a name for himself at the 1956 Democratic convention when he was strongly considered to be the running mate of the party's candidate, Illinois governor Adlai Stevenson. He decided after the convention that he would run for president in 1960, and he became a more active senator, speaking out on foreign policy and serving on the influential Senate Foreign Relations Committee. He was reelected to the Senate in 1958 and announced his candidacy for the presidency in January 1960.

THE 1960 PRESIDENTIAL CAMPAIGN

As the 1960 presidential campaign got underway, the Republican choice was clear. Vice President Richard Nixon had just finished serving eight years with

On January 23, 1960, Swiss oceanographer Jacques Piccard and U.S. naval lieutenant Don Walsh dove seven miles down into the depths of the Pacific Ocean in a vessel called a bathyscaphe. The descent into the Marianas Trench, believed to be the deepest point on Earth, is still the deepest underwater dive ever.

No Roman Catholic had ever been elected president of the United States. Kennedy convinced the voters that he believed strongly in separation of church and state. *(Library of Congress)*

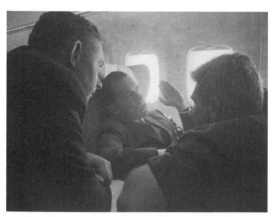

Vice President Richard Nixon discusses campaign strategy with aides. When the 1960 presidential campaign started, Nixon was ahead in most polls. *(Library of Congress)*

President Eisenhower. Eisenhower had sent him around the world to promote U.S. foreign policy and to persuade other countries to choose U.S.-style capitalism rather than communism. Nixon had impressed many Americans by giving Khrushchev a lecture on the virtues of capitalism when he visited the Soviet Union. Nixon chose former Massachusetts senator Henry Cabot Lodge Jr. as his vice-presidential running mate.

The Democratic field was crowded with several candidates. The initial favorite was Senator Hubert Humphrey of Minnesota. As the Democratic primaries unfolded, it became clear that Humphrey's only real challenger was Senator John F. Kennedy of Massachusetts, but Kennedy had a few factors working against him. He had less experience than the other candidates and, at age 43, he was the youngest man ever to run for the presidency. He was also a Roman Catholic, and no Catholic had ever been elected to the presidency.

Kennedy, however, had a lot of money, and he was able to outspend his opponents. His status as a World War II hero and youthful charm and confidence particularly attracted female voters. The nomination boiled down to two primary elections in Wisconsin and West Virginia. Humphrey was well ahead in the polls in both states until Kennedy campaigned in each state, spent money, and charmed the voters. Kennedy won both primaries easily. At the Democratic Convention, Kennedy was nominated on the first ballot. He chose Texas senator Lyndon B. Johnson as his running mate.

The race between Nixon and Kennedy started out with Nixon ahead in the polls. Nixon was more experienced, more conservative, and he had a record of preserving the United States's prosperity and condemning the spread of communism. Kennedy used his youth and vigor to his advantage, telling voters that he would face the 1960s as a challenge full of new opportunities. He called his vision of a new era the New Frontier and embraced the activism of past Democratic presidents, Woodrow Wilson and Franklin Roosevelt. Many voters believed that Kennedy wanted to give the United States a national purpose again, something they thought had been lost in the 1950s.

Two key events swayed the election Kennedy's way. The first was a series of televised debates between the two candidates. Under the bright lights and tough questioning, Kennedy looked much more composed and presidential. Nixon seemed nervous and did not use the cameras well to make contact with the millions of watching voters. The second debate showed that Kennedy's commitment to the civil rights movement was stronger than Nixon's. After the three debates, on October 26, Kennedy called Coretta Scott King, the wife of civil rights leader Martin Luther King Jr. King had been arrested for leading a civil rights protest in Birmingham, Alabama, and was sentenced to four months of hard labor in a southern prison for a previous parole violation. Kennedy told King's wife that he was concerned for her husband's safety and would do what he could to get him out of jail. King was released from jail the next day.

The election was one of the closest in U.S. history, especially as far as the popular vote was concerned. Out of over 68 million votes cast, Kennedy won by only 118,000. A strong African-American vote helped Kennedy carry most of the South, and he won the electoral vote 303 to 219. There were many complaints from Republicans that Kennedy's money was used to buy votes in some states, particularly in Illinois, but Vice President Nixon chose not to ask for a recount, saying it would be bad for the country.

A few weeks after the election, President-elect Kennedy and his wife Jacqueline (Jackie) Bouvier Kennedy attended a performance of the Broadway play *Camelot,* a romantic musical about King Arthur

"There's always the possibility that this madman will do anything."

—Senator (later Vice President) Lyndon Johnson on Soviet premier Khrushchev

"If a free society cannot help the many who are poor, it cannot save the few who are rich."

—President Kennedy in his inaugural address

President Kennedy's speeches inspired young people to get involved in politics and try to solve the challenges facing the new generation. *(Library of Congress)*

On July 21, 1961, Mercury astronaut Virgil "Gus" Grissom became the second American to fly into space. The flight was not a total success because after he exited his space capsule sank into the Atlantic Ocean upon its return, losing valuable research data.

and his knights in the legendary kingdom of Camelot. Journalists immediately referred to Kennedy's youthful administration as the new Camelot. Kennedy preferred to call it the New Frontier. Either way, it was clear the United States was ready for change.

KENNEDY'S NEW FRONTIER

President Kennedy's inauguration speech was one of the most famous ever given. In the address, he issued his famous challenge to Americans, "Ask not what your country can do for you, ask what you can do for your country." Kennedy also said, "The torch has been passed to a new generation of Americans," and he emphasized that action was needed to resolve the two key issues facing the nation: the cold war and civil rights.

Kennedy kept Congress busy during his first year in office, and it passed 33 major pieces of legislation. One of the first programs approved was the Peace Corps, which enabled Americans with particular skills in health care, engineering, and agriculture to volunteer their services to the developing nations of the world. In the past, most U.S. aid to poorer nations was in the form of money, which sometimes wound up in the hands of corrupt leaders. Peace Corps volunteers worked directly with the people, teaching them how to improve their farms, roads, and medical care.

The goal of the Peace Corps was, not only to help some of the poorer populations of the world, but also to convince them to embrace the U.S. capitalism and democracy rather than communism. Although Peace Corps volunteers were paid only their living costs and $1,800 for their two years of duty, Kennedy's call for service was heard. More than 16,000 Americans, mostly young people, volunteered for the program in the first year. In its first five years, the Peace Corps sent more than 10,000 volunteers around the world to provide public service.

Congress approved Kennedy's request for a $300 million increase in welfare payments to needy families with children, and it raised the minimum wage from $1 to $1.25 an hour. It extended unemployment benefits and raised Social Security benefits by $4 million. Two other major Kennedy bills were turned down, however. The president's request for a Medicare program that would guarantee medical care for the elderly and a bill that would grant nearly $6 billion in federal aid to schools were both denied because Congress was concerned about the cost of all the Kennedy programs.

On May 5, 1961, the United States's new Mercury space program, under the direction of the National Aeronautics and Space Administration (NASA), had its first manned flight. Astronaut Alan Shepard was launched into space from Cape Canaveral in Florida. It

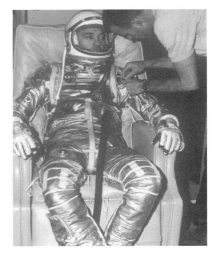

Astronaut Alan Shepard prepares for his flight. *(NASA)*

THE JACKIE LOOK

The Queen Guinevere character in President Kennedy's Camelot was his beautiful young wife Jacqueline, popularly known as Jackie. Only 31 years old when she became first lady, Jackie Kennedy was very popular because of the glamour and culture she brought to the White House. Born into a wealthy family, she had sophisticated tastes in fashion and art and often drew more attention than her husband. After a state visit to France in 1961 the president told the press, "I am the man who accompanied Jackie Kennedy to Paris."

The classic "Jackie look" in fashion was stylish and elegant. She felt she had a responsibility as first lady to wear the best that U.S. fashion had to offer. Several designs became her trademarks: suits with sleeveless blouses, simple pill box hats, bouffant hairdos, and the color pink. For cultural affairs at the White House, Jackie Kennedy brought in a French chef and invited distinguished writers, artists, and musicians. One night in 1962, there was a reception for 49 Nobel Prize winners.

Jackie Kennedy also completely redecorated the White House, which she said she wanted to restore to its former glory. She hired a museum curator and purchased many 19th-century U.S. antiques, including a Dolley Madison sofa and a George Washington mirror. When she finished restoring the mansion, she gave the country a televised tour. Forty-seven million viewers tuned in.

Socialite Jackie Bouvier gave up her newspaper job as the Inquiring Camera Girl to marry Senator John Kennedy in 1953. The storybook wedding was attended by 1,200 guests. *(Library of Congress)*

President Kennedy tours Cape Canaveral. *(NASA)*

was only a 15-minute flight, and even though the Soviet Union had sent one of their cosmonauts into orbit around the earth three weeks earlier, Americans were thrilled. So was President Kennedy. Also in May, he went before Congress and said that he wanted the U.S. space program to make a commitment to land a man on the moon before the decade ended. This announcement showed that Kennedy realized that science was going to be a key weapon in the cold war.

FREEDOM RIDERS IN THE SOUTH

In 1961, the leaders of the civil rights movement looked for a more nationally visible protest to get the federal government involved in their struggle, and they found it in the Freedom Riders. In December 1960, the Supreme Court ruled that segregation in interstate bus terminals was illegal, but most southern terminals ignored the ruling. James Farmer, director of the Congress of Racial Equality (CORE), organized integrated bus trips of both blacks and whites to travel throughout the South. Part of the plan was to have blacks attempt to use the white facilities at every stop. Farmer believed that if violence occurred, the federal government would have to intervene.

The first trouble came in May 1961 in Anniston, Alabama, when a mob of whites smashed the windows, slashed the tires, and firebombed one bus of Freedom Riders. Neither local law enforcement nor the federal government intervened. Another bus suffered a worse fate when it reached Birmingham, Alabama. A large group of whites, led by the local Ku Klux Klan, attacked the Freedom Riders with bats, pipes, and chains, injuring several of them. On May 20, there was a similar attack on a group of 21 Freedom Riders in Montgomery, Alabama, which prompted the U.S. Attorney General

"We've developed a world which is great for everybody but people."

—Playwright Arthur Miller
Commentary on the cold war and American postwar society

Robert Kennedy, the president's brother, to send in U.S. marshals to protect the riders.

Throughout the summer of 1961, Freedom Riders traveled throughout the South challenging segregation. In Mississippi, local authorities filled their jails with the riders, but more kept coming, both black and white. In September, President Kennedy ordered the Interstate Commerce Commission to forbid national bus companies from using segregated terminals. The southern terminals had to integrate or go out of business. It was another small victory for the civil rights movement.

THE CUBAN REVOLUTION AND THE BAY OF PIGS FIASCO

Congress passed a $47 billion defense budget in 1961, the highest peacetime military budget to date. Despite the money and the new president's good intentions, the divisions of the cold war deepened. In President Kennedy's first year in office, the first battleground was Cuba.

Cuba, a Caribbean island lying only 90 miles south of Florida, became a symbol of the communist threat to the United States. In 1959, communist rebel leader Fidel Castro led a revolution that overthrew the corrupt Cuban government of President Fulgencio Batista. Castro immediately seized all foreign properties and businesses, most of them owned by Americans, and installed a communist government. Castro closely aligned Cuba with the Soviet Union and accepted economic and military aid from the Khrushchev regime. He took every opportunity to condemn the United States for its long history of taking advantage of Cuba and supporting the corrupt Batista. He also urged other Latin American countries to embrace communism.

As soon as Castro seized power, the Eisenhower administration worked on plans to remove him, including invasion and assassination. When Kennedy took office, he ordered the Central Intelligence Agency (CIA)

James Farmer founded the civil rights organization CORE in 1942 to help create a society where "race or creed will be neither asset nor handicap." *(Library of Congress)*

U.S. track star **Wilma Rudolph won three gold medals at the 1960 Summer Olympics. This achievement was especially remarkable because Rudolph had contracted polio when she was a child and could not walk unaided for six years.**

Fidel Castro led the revolution to overthrow the dictatorship of Cuba's Fulgencio Batista in 1959. He then immediately cancelled elections and suspended Cuba's constitution. *(Library of Congress)*

On October 23, 1961, the Soviet Union exploded a 50-megaton nuclear bomb, more than twice as powerful as the previous largest bomb. The Soviet bomb had 2,500 times the explosive power of the atomic bomb that destroyed Hiroshima in World War II. It temporarily increased the world's radioactive debris by 30 percent.

to continue to work on these plans. In the atmosphere of the cold war, Kennedy insisted that it was unacceptable for a communist nation so close to the United States to receive military aid from the Soviet Union. To counteract Castro's influence, Kennedy created the Alliance for Progress, in which Latin American countries received significant economic aid from the United States if they rejected communism.

On April 17, 1961, Kennedy approved a CIA plan to invade Cuba from the Bay of Pigs on its southern coast and assassinate Castro. The plan was a disaster from the start. Castro knew the invasion was coming. The 1,500 U.S.-trained Cuban exiles were met by 20,000 Cuban troops and newly imported Soviet artillery. The plan to kill Castro using an assassin from the Mafia (a group of organized crime families and their associates) also never had a chance. Two days later, 114 Cuban exiles and 4 Americans were dead. Kennedy went on television to apologize to the U.S. public for the fiasco. Americans forgave Kennedy, but Castro and the Soviets did not. The failed invasion caused the Soviet Union to send more military aid to Cuba, and led to a showdown the world had never seen before.

BERLIN: COLD WAR HOT SPOT

The other cold war battleground was in Berlin, Germany. After Germany's defeat in World War II, the nation was divided into two sections: East Germany was firmly controlled by the Soviet Union, and West Germany was controlled by the Allies (the United States, Britain, and France). Germany's capital, Berlin, was divided in a similar way. During the 1950s, West Germany and West Berlin flourished and were gradually granted self-rule by the former Allies, but U.S. troops remained in West Berlin, which was located in the heart of East Germany. The Soviet Union kept a tight grip on East Germany, and both the economy and freedom suffered there. Between

Scientists such as Dr. Mark Mills testified before Congress on the dangers of atomic radioactive fallout such as that created by the Soviet Union's 1961 test. *(Library of Congress)*

1949 and 1961, nearly 3 million people left East Germany for West Germany by crossing the border between East and West Berlin. Losing so many East Germans to the West was an embarrassment to the Soviet Union and a drain on the East German economy.

Throughout 1961, and particularly after President Kennedy's blunder in the Bay of Pigs invasion, Khrushchev demanded that Berlin become one city under communist rule. He contended that the existence of U.S. troops so close to Soviet-controlled territory was an invitation to war, possibly nuclear war. Kennedy would not remove the troops, and during the summer of 1961, the city was a dangerous symbol of the cold war.

In August, Khrushchev decided Berlin was not worth a war and found an unusual solution to his problem of East German emigration. He had a wall of concrete and barbed-wire built along a 28-mile border between the two Berlins. He said it was to protect the East from U.S. attack, but a series of traps and ditches

"Such tests not only contaminate the atmosphere but the hearts and minds of people everywhere."

—India's prime minister Jawaharlal Nehru on the testing of nuclear weapons by the world's nuclear powers

FALLOUT SHELTERS

Out of President Kennedy's $47 billion defense budget for his first year in office, $207 million was designated for a fallout shelter program. The government identified buildings and other underground areas as shelters where Americans were to go for protection from radiation in case of a nuclear attack. These shelters were stocked with food, water, medicine, and other supplies. Fallout shelter signs appeared in most communities that pointed the way and indicated the capacity of the shelters. Two large underground shelters were built outside Washington, D.C., one for Congress and one for the president and his staff.

After the Bay of Pigs disaster in Cuba, President Kennedy urged Americans to construct fallout shelters in their homes. Some families merely reinforced the walls of their basements and stocked them with supplies considered necessary to survive after a nuclear attack. Americans were told that two weeks of supplies would probably be enough, and sales of canned goods, first aid kits, and toilet paper had a brief boom.

Shelter builders also had a good year as companies offered to construct facilities to suit every budget. Extras included televisions, pool tables, bars, and fake windows on the walls to make them seem more like home. Some of the professional shelters were so well furnished that families used them as recreation rooms while waiting for the bombs of World War III to fall.

One optimistic magazine article predicted that 97 percent of Americans protected by a shelter would survive a nuclear war. Scientists later concluded that this survival rate was a misguided illusion. They acknowledged that such a war is likely to cause a nuclear winter, in which freezing temperatures, darkness, and radiation make life impossible for thousands of years. The only way to survive a nuclear war is to prevent it.

The Polaroid instant camera made its debut in 1960. After a user took a picture, a fully developed black and white photo came out of the camera one minute later.

on the east side of the wall made it clear that the wall was to prevent East Germans from leaving. Many East Germans continued to flee despite the danger. The Berlin Wall averted a military confrontation in the area, but it also kept families separated and stood for several decades as an unpleasant reminder of a dangerous time in cold war history.

LITERATURE IN THE 1960S

Many new voices appeared in U.S. literature during the 1960s, and these writers took on some of the difficult issues troubling many Americans. Like other aspects of the 1960s counterculture, the stage for the literature of the 1960s was set in 1957 when Jack Kerouac's *On the Road* was published. The book's theme of a generation's rejection of traditional values fit the 1960s perfectly.

Many books of the 1960s protested aspects of U.S. society. Ken Kesey's *One Flew Over the Cuckoo's Nest* (1962) used the setting of a mental institution to condemn, not only the treatment of the mentally ill in the United States, but also the general repression of creativity by those in authority. The novel's hero, Randle Patrick McMurphy, is a nonconformist patient who uses a humane approach toward his fellow inmates to create an atmosphere of support and joy. The head nurse is a rigid disciplinarian who believes in schedules more than treatments. The cuckoo's nest refers to the hospital as a whole. Its reaction to the patients' new, more lively attitude is to administer shock treatments and lobotomies, or brain surgery, to stop their outbursts.

Joseph Heller uses a World War II setting to condemn the U.S. political and military system in *Catch-22* (1961). The no-win situation, which defines the Catch-22 principle in the novel, becomes clear when the hero pilot, John Yossarian, tries to avoid insane orders that would result in his death by claiming that he is insane. His military doctor, however, says that Yossarian's refusal to carry out the orders proves his sanity. The only way to prove insanity is to carry out the insane orders. Unable to deal with the irrational system, the hero deserts the military.

Kurt Vonnegut wrote some of the decade's most experimental novels, including *Mother Night* (1961), *Cat's Cradle* (1963), and *God Bless You, Mr. Rosewater* (1965), as well as one of the decade's most ambitious antiwar novels, *Slaughterhouse Five* (1969). Young readers appreciated Vonnegut's themes and his experiments with the novel's structure as the hero Billy Pilgrim travels through time and jumps among three different realities. At one point, Vonnegut has time run backward, as when World War II soldiers return home alive and Nazi leader Adolf Hitler becomes an innocent baby.

The most popular book to come out of the decade was probably Harper Lee's *To Kill a Mockingbird* (1960). The novel is a literary masterpiece and an indictment of U.S. racism. The novel won a Pulitzer Prize in 1961 and has become a mainstay of high-school English courses.

Norman Mailer's *Armies of the Night* won both the Pulitzer Prize and the National Book Award in 1969. *(Library of Congress)*

On August 16, 1960, as part of the U.S. space program U.S. Air Force Captain Joseph Kittinger set a record for the highest high-altitude parachute jump by falling 102,800 feet or nearly 20 miles. His body reached a speed of 614 mph and broke the sound barrier before he returned safely to Earth.

Tom Wolfe was one of the innovators of the 1960s New Journalism, whose writers used the techniques of fiction in writing nonfiction books on contemporary issues. *(Library of Congress)*

The most popular dance song of 1961 was African-American singer Chubby Checker's "The Twist."
It started a dance craze that led to other new dances, such as the Locomotion, the Mashed Potatoes, the Pony, and the Jerk.

The story deals with sister and brother Scout and Jem Finch growing up in Alabama during the depression. During their summer vacation, the children become fascinated by their mysterious neighbor Boo Radley and the trial of Tom Robinson, a black man. Boo has not been seen by townsfolk for many years, and he is supposedly a dangerous maniac. Robinson has been unjustly accused of raping a poor white farmer's daughter. The children's lawyer father, Atticus Finch, defends Robinson. The wise, just, and morally strong Atticus becomes Lee's symbol of what Americans should be like.

A new form of writing, known as personal journalism, became very popular during the 1960s. This genre included nonfiction stories written in the form of a novel. The most noteworthy example was Truman Capote's *In Cold Blood* (1966) about the senseless 1959 murders of a Kansas farmer and his family. Norman Mailer's *Armies of the Night* (1968) about Mailer's participation in the 1967 antiwar demonstration at the Pentagon was another popular nonfiction novel. Another important example of this genre was Tom Wolfe's *The Electric Kool-Aid Acid Test* (1968), which recounts the wild adventures of novelist Ken Kesey. In 1964, Kesey purchased a 1939 bus, painted it bright colors, and set off with a group of friends called the Merry Pranksters. Along the way, Kesey and the Pranksters staged several "happenings," (special performances unique to the 1960s) that included drug use, members of the Hell's Angels (a nationwide motorcycle gang), rock music, dancing, and strobe lights.

CHAPTER 3

CRISIS AND ASSASSINATION, 1962–1963

DURING PRESIDENT JOHN F. KENNEDY'S second year in office, the cold war escalated to the most dangerous moment in U.S. history, but 1962 began with a triumph in the space program. On February 20, astronaut John Glenn became the first American to orbit the earth. It was only a three-orbit trip of five hours, but it was a symbolic victory for the United States because it brought the U.S. space program closer to the Soviet Union's accomplishments.

John Glenn (center) returned from his space mission a hero and later served 24 years in the U.S. Senate. He returned to space in 1998 aboard the space shuttle at the age of 77. *(NASA)*

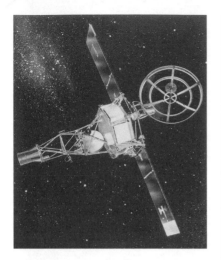

Mariner 2 was the first successful interplanetary spacecraft. It measured the temperature of Venus's surface at nearly 900 degrees Fahrenheit. *(NASA)*

"Anybody who would spend $40 billion in a race to the moon for national prestige is nuts."

—Former president Eisenhower on the cost of the space program

Two months later, astronaut Scott Carpenter duplicated Glenn's achievement. In July, *Telstar 1,* the first commercial communications satellite, was launched, enabling live television broadcasts to be transmitted around the world. In October, astronaut Walter Schirra completed a space flight of six orbits around the earth. It did not seem to matter that the Soviet Union launched two cosmonauts in August. Americans began to believe that their country could win the race to put a person on the moon by the end of the decade. Congress apparently agreed, as it passed Kennedy's $2.4 billion space budget for 1963.

The spending helped the United States push past the Soviet Union in the space race in 1963. The Soviet Union continued to have success with long orbital missions, but an unmanned mission to Mars to take photos failed. (Not all Soviet missions were led by male cosmonauts; a female cosmonaut was part of one flight.) Meanwhile the United States's *Mariner 2* to Venus passed within 25,000 miles of the planet, sending back extensive information. In May 1963, the highly successful Mercury space program ended when astronaut Gordon Cooper completed a 22-orbit, 34-hour mission around the earth.

THE CUBAN MISSILE CRISIS

The failure of the Bay of Pigs invasion did not deter the Kennedy administration from making plans to oust the communist leader Fidel Castro of Cuba. Throughout 1962, Kennedy's military advisers and the CIA worked on various schemes, but they included a direct invasion of the island by U.S. troops. Kennedy wanted Castro overthrown, but he continued to reject a direct invasion because he feared it would trigger a nuclear confrontation between the United States and the Soviet Union, Cuba's sworn ally.

Kennedy decided to move slowly and took two steps in early 1962. In February, he declared Cuba to be an out-

Photos like this from American U-2 spy planes revealed that Russia was supplying Cuba with nuclear weapons capable of striking U.S. cities. *(U.S. Air Force)*

law state and authorized a full embargo on all U.S.-Cuban trade. He also authorized a war exercise in the Caribbean Sea, which tested U.S. naval readiness in preparation for an invasion of Cuba. In April, Kennedy made another key decision that would have a huge effect on upcoming events. He authorized the placement of nuclear weapons in Turkey, near the Turkish-Soviet border.

Khrushchev was furious about the U.S. missiles in Turkey, and both Cuba and the Soviet Union were convinced a U.S. invasion of Cuba was imminent, especially after they learned about the U.S. naval exercise. In May, Castro agreed to accept an offer from the Soviet Union to have its nuclear missiles placed on Cuban territory. Castro and the Soviets argued about who would have final control over their use, but by July, the missiles were secretly being shipped to Cuba.

Throughout August and September, Soviet freighters continued to make deliveries to Cuba for the missile site. U.S. intelligence, gathered mostly from U-2 spy planes, confirmed that the missiles were being set up in Cuba, but it could not determine at first whether they were defensive rather than offensive weapons, and therefore not a direct threat to the United States.

THE OTHER AMERICA

After the Cuban missile crisis revealed the folly and danger of the cold war, President Kennedy decided to fight a different war. He intended to make the war against poverty the theme of his 1964 reelection campaign. Kennedy had seen poverty up close during his first campaign, especially in West Virginia. He had also read a book on poverty in the United States that strongly affected him, titled *The Other America* (1962) by Michael Harrington.

Harrington said that despite the increased affluence of many Americans over the previous decade, there was also increased poverty. Harrington estimated that 40 to 50 million people, out of a total U.S. population of 180 million, lived in poverty, yet the majority of Americans did not seem to notice. He claimed that one reason the poor in the United States had become invisible was racism. In the South, segregation had deprived African Americans of a decent education and good jobs, so they moved to the North's urban areas during the Great Migration of the 1920s, 1930s, and 1940s. But changing economic conditions, including the growth of the suburbs in the 1950s, made good jobs scarce. African Americans often found themselves in the ghettos of the big cities, again segregated from the mainstream of U.S. society, this time because of their poverty.

Harrington stated that the government acted on behalf of the poor during the Great Depression because the poverty had spread into the white middle class. This middle class had a voice through their labor unions and their votes. However, the new poor, mostly black, were not only invisible, they also had no voice. In the early 1960s, white Americans were enjoying affluence, often living in the suburbs where there were no poor people in sight. They thought poverty was a problem from the past. Harrington's book, television news, and the civil rights movement started to open people's eyes. Kennedy proposed an economic plan that targeted poverty. He would not live to see the plan enacted, but his successor would start the war on poverty for him.

On Christmas Eve in 1962, Cuba released 1,113 prisoners captured in the 1961 Bay of Pigs invasion in return for $50 million in medicine and food from the United States.

Throughout the tense summer, the Soviet Union repeatedly assured the Kennedy administration that the weapons were defensive.

On October 16, photos from a U-2 mission confirmed that the missiles were offensive ballistic nuclear missiles with a range of up to 2,500 miles, which could attack most of the continental United States. The Kennedy administration kept this news from Americans and debated for several days over the correct response. Kennedy and all his advisers agreed the missiles had to be removed, but all military plans seemed to carry the risk of nuclear war. His military advisers argued for an air strike to destroy the weapons, but they could not guarantee that all the missiles would be destroyed before one or more were launched.

Against the advice of the military, Kennedy decided to impose a naval blockade around Cuba, stopping all further shipments of Soviet missiles and military equipment to the Cuban missile sites. He also intended to present the U-2 photos at a session of the United Nations, to pressure the Soviet Union to remove the existing missiles. On October 22, Kennedy went on television to inform Americans about the crisis. The entire nation held its breath. A poll showed that most Americans expected nuclear war, and some headed for their fallout shelters. Khrushchev gave orders for the Soviet ships to continue on course, but when they reached the U.S. Navy's ships at the blockade line, they stopped and turned back.

Over the next couple of days, the United States's UN ambassador, Adlai Stevenson, presented proof of the existence of the missiles to the United Nations and publicly embarrassed the Soviet leadership for their lies. Finally, Khrushchev agreed to remove the nuclear missiles if the United States promised not to invade Cuba and to remove its nuclear missiles from Turkey within six months. (The U.S. agreement to remove the missiles from Turkey was not revealed until many years later. Kennedy had concealed this part of the agreement because he did not want it to seem as if the United States had altered policy as a result of a nuclear threat.) On November 2, President Kennedy announced that the dismantling of the missiles on Cuba had begun and the world breathed more easily. Kennedy said there were no victors, only survivors.

THE NUCLEAR TEST BAN TREATY

The cold war between the United States and the Soviet Union continued for many more years, but, after the Cuban missile crisis, but both sides realized that the first steps had to be taken to reduce the threat of nuclear war. Two important agreements were reached in the summer of 1963 to achieve that goal. The first was the Nuclear Test Ban Treaty.

Representatives of the United States and the Soviet Union had been discussing nuclear test bans, arms

U.S. biologist Rachel Carson's *Silent Spring* was published in 1962. One of the first books to warn of the dangers of environmental pollution, it helped lead the way to the banning of the pesticide DDT.

Rachel Carson worked for the U.S. Fish and Wildlife Service until the success of *Silent Spring* let her retire and write full-time. (*U.S. Fish and Wildlife Service*)

"It is always the brave and the best who die."

—President Kennedy in the letter of condolence to the family of Major Rudolph Anderson, the only casualty of the Cuban missile crisis

"I am prepared to wait until hell freezes over if that's your decision and I'm also prepared to present evidence in this room."

—U.S. ambassador to the United Nations Adlai Stevenson, speaking to the Soviet ambassador who refused to answer his question about whether the Soviet Union had placed nuclear weapons in Cuba

The nuclear submarine USS *Thresher* sank off the coast of Massachusetts on April 10, 1963, claiming 129 lives. The wreckage was later located 8,500 feet under the Atlantic Ocean, but the cause of the sinking was never determined.

control, and mutual disarmament since 1958 but without success. Frightened by the events in Cuba, the two sides agreed to step up their meetings immediately. The talks dragged on. Khrushchev agreed to disarmament, but he refused the mutual inspections the United States wanted to verify Soviet actions. The lack of trust on both sides made any disarmament agreement impossible. Kennedy then pressed for arms control talks to limit the use of nuclear weapons, but Khrushchev wanted to wait until a test ban treaty could be worked out.

The Nuclear Test Ban Treaty was signed on August 5, 1963. It was a small first step, but both sides agreed that the harmful radiation from nuclear tests was bad for the entire world. By this time, around 400 nuclear devices had been tested–259 by the United States, 126 by the Soviet Union, and the remainder by Britain and France. The earth's atmosphere was becoming increasingly polluted with radioactive debris, especially near the test sites where isolated populations lived. The Test Ban Treaty forbade all further nuclear testing in the atmosphere, in outer space, and underwater. Arms negotiators did not reach an agreement on underground testing because there was no technology available to verify whether a nation was complying with the treaty. One hundred other nations also signed the treaty, with France and China being two notable exceptions.

The other step taken to reduce the nuclear threat was the installment of a telephone hotline between the White House in Washington, D.C., and the Kremlin in Moscow. The line enabled leaders from the world's two superpowers to communicate instantly about future crises as a means of preventing nuclear confrontation. The threat of nuclear war was still present, but the two steps showed that the United States and the Soviet Union could cooperate.

Kennedy wanted to devote the rest of his first term to domestic issues, particularly civil rights, the economy, and a new war on poverty. Events in Southeast Asia, however, distracted him and proved that the world was still burdened with cold war conflicts.

SOUTHEAST ASIA: NEW BATTLEGROUNDS

On October 20, 1962, as the Cuban Missile Crisis was at its height, China invaded India, its neighbor, over a border dispute that had been simmering for several years. With the United States and the Soviet Union on the edge of nuclear war, the world paid little notice to the border war, especially after it ended in a cease-fire one month later. However, it was an indication of growing conflicts throughout Southeast Asia. With issues in Cuba and Berlin fairly settled, Southeast Asia became the new cold war battleground.

Indonesia's president, Achmad Sukarno, became a vocal opponent of both the United States and the

American troops in Vietnam in the early 1960s, like these near Dak To, were supposed to be advisers. As the war escalated, however, they became more involved in combat. *(U.S. Army)*

President Sukarno of Indonesia became his nation's first president in 1945. He was all smiles when he visited Washington, D.C., in 1956, but he later became strongly anti-American. *(Library of Congress)*

In an exchange of political prisoners on February 10, 1962, the Soviet Union released U.S. pilot Gary Powers, and the United States released Soviet spy Rudolf Abel. Powers had been shot down over the Soviet Union in 1960 and had been sentenced to 10 years imprisonment for espionage.

Soviet Union. He called on other Asian, African, and Latin American countries to follow his so-called Guided Democracy policy, which rejected alliance with either superpower. His speeches were particularly anti-U.S. because he resented U.S. interference in Indonesian affairs. Sukarno was also threatening to invade the neighboring island of West Irian to remove the Dutch colonial rulers there. Such a war would undoubtedly involve the United States, a sworn defensive ally of the Netherlands. The issue was settled when Sukarno agreed to tone down his anti-U.S. speeches in return for some U.S. aid and a Dutch withdrawal from West Irian the following year.

Other battles were not as easy to settle. In Laos, the Southeast Asian country bordering Vietnam, civil war had existed since France granted the colony its independence in 1954. The war became a struggle between Laotian pro-communists and pro-U.S. Laotians, in which each side received military aid from its corresponding superpower. Kennedy wanted to stop the communists from taking power, but he did not want U.S. troops involved. He successfully negotiated a cease-fire in Laos in 1961. The cease-fire did not hold, and the civil war spread to Thailand's border. In 1962, Kennedy sent 4,000 U.S. troops to the Thailand–Laos border to try to stop the spread of the war.

The most troublesome conflict remained in Vietnam, where Kennedy faced two problems. First, communist forces from North Vietnam were now well-equipped by both the Soviet Union and China. Second, the corrupt South Vietnamese President Ngo Dinh Diem was losing the support of his people. In 1962, $300 million in U.S. aid and an increase in U.S. troops to 11,000 had only helped maintain a stalemate. U.S. troops were not supposed to be involved in combat, but 25 Americans died in battles during the year.

In 1963, Diem's harsh, ineffective leadership led to his demise. First, Diem attempted to limit the growth of the Viet Cong forces in South Vietnam by isolating rural villages and relocating the residents to government-controlled internment camps. He then conscripted (drafted) many young men into the army and returned land to wealthy landowners from the French colonial era.

During Buddhist demonstrations against Diem in May 1963, South Vietnamese police killed nine demonstrators. In June, Buddhist monks protested Diem's rule by burning themselves to death in the streets of Saigon, the capital of South Vietnam. As these suicidal protests continued, a desperate Diem sent troops to attack several Buddhist temples, and 1,400 monks were arrested. By November, even the Kennedy administration could no longer support the pro-U.S. Diem. With Kennedy's approval, a military coup overthrew Diem on November 1–2. Diem and several of his top aides were killed in the coup. Unfortunately, the coup only made South Vietnam more unstable as no strong leader stepped forward to take Diem's place.

By the end of 1963, the United States was spending $400 million a year in Vietnam and had more than 16,000 troops there. Congressional opposition to U.S. Vietnam policy also started in 1963 as the Democratic Senate majority leader Mike Mansfield argued against U.S. participation in the war.

GAINING PRESIDENTIAL SUPPORT FOR CIVIL RIGHTS

After the success of the sit-ins and Freedom Riders of 1961, the civil rights movement experienced an unusual stalemate for the first half of 1962. Martin Luther King Jr. and his Southern Christian Leadership Conference (SCLC) were asked to join a civil rights movement in Albany, Georgia, to protest the town's segregation laws. He brought many supporters to Georgia with him and led many demonstrations in what came to be called the Albany Movement. The local police

On June 15, 1962, members of the political organization Students for a Democratic Society (SDS) issued their Port Huron Statement proclaiming their demands for more social programs, rights legislation, and an end to the cold war. The statement is usually thought of as the beginning of the student movement of the 1960s.

The Kennedy administration was a strong supporter of the civil rights movement. Above, Attorney General Robert Kennedy addresses a group of demonstrators in Washington, D.C. *(Library of Congress)*

chief Laurie Pritchett, however, decided to fight nonviolence with nonviolence. Pritchett and the police force arrested the demonstrators over and over, including King three times, but Pritchett insisted on nonviolence from his men as strongly as King did from his followers.

Pritchett had the demonstrators arrested without incident, and as soon as Albany's jails were filled, the protestors were released. When King and other SCLC leaders refused to pay bail, Pritchett had them released anyway, saying an anonymous donor had put up the money. The strategy worked. Without hostile confrontation and violence, there was little television coverage and no white support. As a result, the Kennedy administration had no reason to get involved. Frustrated by the lack of progress, King asked President Kennedy to issue a second emancipation proclamation (President Abraham Lincoln issued the first one) as a show of support for the civil rights movement, but the president declined.

The president's refusal proved only a temporary setback, however. Two events sparked the movement once again. In August 1963, the activists in the Albany Movement spread out across Georgia to organize voter registration drives in African-American communities. This approach was strongly supported by Attorney General Robert Kennedy, who knew the untapped political power held by the huge numbers of unregistered black voters. The organizers were confronted with Ku Klux Klan (KKK)–organized violence throughout the state. KKK supporters assaulted activists and bombed or burned black churches where the drives took place. This time President Kennedy intervened; he promised federal protection for all voter registration drives across Georgia.

The other triggering event was African-American James Meredith's attempt to enroll in the all-white University of Mississippi in Oxford. Meredith had spent nine years in the U.S. Air Force. He had showed up at the university twice with court papers ordering his

James Meredith's integration of the University of Mississippi is an example of how the civil rights movement was often based on the courageous actions of an individual. *(Library of Congress)*

"I'm not afraid of dying. If I die, it would be for a good cause. I've been fighting for America just as much as the soldiers in Vietnam."

—Civil rights leader Medgar Evers, who was killed by a Ku Klux Klan member in 1963

entrance into the university. Both times the segregationist governor of Mississippi, Ross Barnett, personally refused him admission. Finally, on September 30, Meredith showed up with a court order from Supreme Court justice Hugo Black. Kennedy sent 3,000 U.S. troops and 400 U.S. Marshals to support him.

Meredith was able to register, but that night, thousands of white students and city residents rioted on the campus and in the city. The riot lasted for 15 hours and left two people dead, 70 injured, and 200 arrested. During the riot, Mississippi's state police were ordered by the governor to stay home. The next day, however, a heavily guarded Meredith attended his first day of classes at the University of Mississippi.

In many ways, 1963 proved to be the most critical year in the civil rights struggle. In April, King took the SCLC to Birmingham, Alabama, where he knew the police chief, Bull Connor, would provide the confrontation and publicity the movement needed. As the demonstrations started, television audiences saw the peaceful protestors attacked with clubs, police dogs, and high-pressure fire hoses. There were also 1,300 arrests. And, during a children's march, Connor used police dogs and arrested dozens of children.

School integration was accomplished without incident in some places. Above, students at Anacostia High School in Washington, D.C., learn together peacefully. *(Library of Congress)*

King and the civil rights movement were often met by violence in the South. The Gaston Motel in Birmingham, Alabama, was bombed during King's stay there in 1963. *(Library of Congress)*

As the situation worsened, some demonstrators dismissed King's pleas for nonviolence and threw bricks and bottles at Connor's forces. Robert Kennedy and his civil rights staff went to Alabama to try to turn the direction of the protest toward voter registration, but it did not work. After Birmingham mayor Arthur Haynes called the staffers "a bunch of gutless traitors," the KKK went on a rampage, bombing King's brother's home and the demonstrators' motel headquarters. An ensuing riot left 50 more people injured.

By June, the battle had spread to the University of Alabama in Tuscaloosa, where the strongly segregationist governor George Wallace was blocking the doors to prevent the admission of two black students. When the governor would not move away at the direction of Assistant Attorney General Nicholas Katzenbach, Kennedy put the Alabama National Guard under federal control to enforce the law. Wallace backed off, the students gained admission, and the situation became another hard-earned victory for civil rights.

Southern governors often defied federal integration laws. Federal troops finally made Governor Wallace allow African-American students to enter the University of Alabama. *(Library of Congress)*

That night, President Kennedy went on national television and gave his strongest support yet to the movement. He said that the United States was a nation that "will not be fully free until all its citizens are free," and he demanded legislative action in the states and in Congress to ensure freedom for all. Within days, he had submitted a sweeping civil rights bill to Congress. The bill not only made segregation illegal at all levels but also called for tougher voting rights legislation and nearly $2 billion in job training. The night after Kennedy's television appearance, civil rights leader Medgar Evers was shot to death in Jackson, Mississippi.

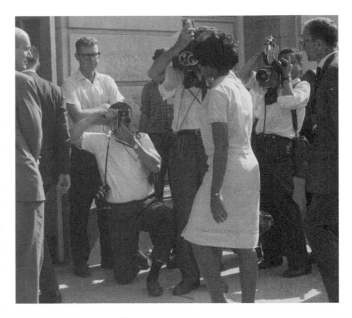

The National Guard and U.S. Attorney General Nicholas Katzenbach escort Vivian Malone into the University of Alabama, ending 132 years of segregation at the school. *(Library of Congress)*

In August, black leaders, including King, organized a huge march in Washington, D.C., in support of Kennedy's civil rights bill. More than 200,000 Americans, including about 30,000 whites, gathered in front of the Lincoln Memorial in the largest protest the capital had ever seen. The demonstration remained

Civil rights leaders and marchers voice their demands during the 1963 March on Washington. *(Library of Congress)*

The civil rights movement included many issues. Demonstrators at the August 1963 March on Washington call for equal rights, integrated schools, decent housing, and an end to bias. *(Library of Congress)*

A newspaper headline reads "They're Pouring in from All Over" as 200,000 demonstrators gathered in front of the Lincoln Memorial during the 1963 March on Washington. *(Library of Congress)*

peaceful as the crowd sang the movement's new theme song "We Shall Overcome," and listened to speeches. The highlight came with King's stirring and hopeful "I Have a Dream" speech.

King's speech was important because it emphasized that Americans' dream of freedom and equality was an issue of creating laws and changing the attitude of Americans. Just two weeks after King's speech, however, there was a bombing in Birmingham, Alabama. An African-American church, which was used as a headquarters for civil rights workers, was destroyed, killing four people and injuring 20. The people killed were 11- to 14-year-old girls attending Sunday school.

Kennedy's civil rights bill finally passed Congress in 1964. Yet changing the minds and hearts of some Americans would prove even more difficult than passing civil rights legislation.

THE NEW FRONTIER ENDS

As President Kennedy's second year in office came to a close, he had to start thinking about the 1964 election. He was still very popular and had shown strong leadership qualities when dealing with the cold war and civil rights.

"I HAVE A DREAM"

The following excerpt is the conclusion of Martin Luther King Jr.'s famous speech, which he delivered during the March on Washington in 1963.

Demonstrators at the 1963 March on Washington line the Reflecting Pool overlooking the Washington Monument in the distance.
(Library of Congress)

. . . I have a dream that one day this nation will rise up and live out the true meaning of its creed: "We hold these truths to be self-evident, that all men are created equal." I have a dream that one day on the red hills of Georgia, the sons of former slaves and the sons of former slave owners will be able to sit down together at a table of brotherhood. I have a dream that one day even the state of Mississippi, sweltering with the heat of injustice and oppression, will be transformed into an oasis of freedom and justice. I have a dream that my four children will one day live in a nation where they will not be judged by the color of their skin but by the content of their character. I have a dream today...

...This will be the day when all of God's children will be able to sing with new meaning: "My country, 'tis of thee, sweet land of liberty, of thee I sing. Land where my fathers died, land of the pilgrim's pride, from every mountainside, let freedom ring." And if America is to be a great nation, this must become true. So let freedom ring from the prodigious hilltops of New Hampshire. Let freedom ring from the mighty mountains of New York. Let freedom ring from the heightening Alleghenies of Pennsylvania! Let freedom ring from the snowcapped Rockies of Colorado! Let freedom ring from the curvaceous slopes of California! But not only that: let freedom ring from Stone Mountain of Georgia! Let freedom ring from Lookout Mountain of Tennessee! Let freedom ring from every hill and every molehill of Mississippi. From every mountainside, let freedom ring.

When we let freedom ring, when we let it ring from every village and every hamlet, from every state and every city, we will be able to speed up that day when all of God's children, black men and white men, Jews and Gentiles, Protestants and Catholics, will be able to join hands and sing in the words of the old Negro spiritual, "Free at last! Free at last! Thank God Almighty, we are free at last!"

The economy was very strong. The Peace Corps, the space program, and other forward-looking projects had inspired a young generation to pursue public service. He knew he had also made some enemies, especially in the South, with his support of the civil rights movement.

In November 1963, President and Mrs. Kennedy visited Texas, a key state in the upcoming election. Despite warnings that Dallas was dangerous, anti-Kennedy territory, the president included the city on his campaign tour of the state. On November 22, as the president rode in a motorcade through the streets of Dallas, he was shot

Vice President Johnson is sworn in aboard *Air Force One,* the presidential plane, after President Kennedy's assassination in Dallas. A stunned Jackie Kennedy stands at his side. *(Lyndon Baines Johnson Library and Museum)*

"We'll laugh again. It's just that we'll never be young again."

—President Kennedy's assistant secretary of Labor Daniel Patrick Moynihan, after the assassination of the president

and killed by an assassin, Lee Harvey Oswald. Texas governor John Connally was also wounded by the gunfire.

The apparent reason for Kennedy's assassination was Oswald's strong communist and pro-Castro feelings. Two days later, with millions watching on live television as Oswald was being transferred to a higher security jail, he was shot by nightclub owner Jack Ruby. Ruby claimed he was simply angry at Oswald, but the strange circumstances surrounding the horrible events of Dallas led many to think a conspiracy was behind the president's death. Some of the suspects in these conspiracy theories included the CIA, the FBI, the Mafia, the military, Castro, and even Vice President Lyndon Johnson. A commission investigation led by Chief Justice Earl Warren, however, later concluded that Oswald had acted alone in the assassination.

Vice President Johnson was sworn in as the nation's new president. Stunned Americans watched on television as President Kennedy was buried in Arlington National Cemetery. It was a critical moment in 20th-century U.S. history, and most Americans were aware of it. Even Kennedy's detractors admitted the president had commitment, energy, and a hopeful view of the country's future. People agreed that he had inspired many of the nation's young people. Many Americans struggled with a strong sense of loss and confusion in the days after the president's death, and they wondered if they could regain their hope in the future. The turbulent events of the rest of the decade had their roots in that struggle.

CHAPTER 4

THE GREAT SOCIETY, 1964–1965

President Johnson was able to work well with Congress as soon as he took office. Much of his legislation was approved, and bill signings in the White House became common. *(Library of Congress)*

D URING THE 1960 PRESIDENTIAL election, John F. Kennedy said that Senator Lyndon B. Johnson was the next best candidate after himself. The two Democratic senators were devoted admirers of President Franklin Roosevelt's New Deal, and they agreed on most domestic and foreign policy issues. However, their backgrounds and styles were very different.

Johnson was born on a poor farm near Stonewall, Texas, on August 27, 1908, but his father was much more interested in politics than farming. The farm

Lyndon Johnson (at podium) had the support of President Roosevelt during his 1941 Senate campaign, but he would lose a very close election. *(Lyndon Baines Johnson Library and Museum)*

In January 1964, the U.S. surgeon general, Luther Terry, announced that cigarette smoking could lead to cancer, heart disease, and lung disease. Despite the warning, cigarette smoking increased over the next several years.

failed, and the family moved to the small town of Johnson City, where Johnson's father became a businessman and served five terms in the Texas state legislature. Johnson graduated from Southwest Texas State Teachers College in 1930 and accepted a job as a teacher of public speaking at Sam Houston High School in Houston.

After just one year of teaching, he was offered a political job as assistant to Texas member of Congress Richard Kleberg. Johnson arrived in Washington D.C., in 1932 and became a strong supporter of Roosevelt's New Deal policies. Johnson won a congressional seat in 1937 and established a reputation as a politician who knew how to get things done, especially for the people he represented. Johnson believed in bipartisan politics: He sought the middle ground of popular opinion on legislation and thus often gained the support of both Democrats and Republicans. Despite his success in the House, Johnson lost an attempt at a Senate seat in 1941.

Like Kennedy, Johnson served bravely in World War II in the Pacific, and he earned a Silver Star medal. After the war, Johnson again set his sights on the Senate and in 1948, he won one of the closest senatorial races ever by only 87 votes. Johnson was easily reelected in 1954, and throughout his two terms in the Senate, he continued his policy of bipartisan politics, often supporting the Republican administration of President Eisenhower. Johnson called it "the politics of responsibility." However, Johnson was also a strong supporter of the military and opposed Eisenhower's cuts in defense spending.

Johnson's power rose quickly in the Senate and he became the Senate majority leader in 1953. The Speaker of the House at the time was Sam Rayburn, an old friend of Johnson's father, and the two Texans ruled Congress for the rest of the decade. Johnson and Rayburn were especially influential because President Eisenhower believed it was Congress's job to determine policy, not the president's. As majority leader, Johnson was able to get a weak, but symbolic civil rights bill passed in 1957, and he continued his strong support of defense by speeding up the U.S. missile program after the Soviet Union's success with *Sputnik*.

By 1956, Johnson's name was being mentioned as a possible presidential candidate, and he was nominated at the 1956 Democratic convention. Johnson also supported Kennedy's bid for the vice-presidential nomination at this convention. Neither Johnson nor Kennedy won, but they had set themselves up as the frontrunners for the 1960 campaign.

As the 1960 campaign developed, several Democratic senators, including Kennedy, were actively campaigning. Johnson decided to be a candidate but remained in the Senate fulfilling his duties as majority leader instead of campaigning. He thought a deadlocked convention would cause the Democratic delegates to turn to him when none of the other candidates had enough votes to win the nomination. The strategy did not work, as Kennedy won the nomination on the first ballot. Kennedy chose Johnson as his vice-presidential running mate, and the ticket narrowly defeated the Republican Nixon-Lodge ticket for the White House.

Kennedy's closest presidential adviser was his brother Attorney General Robert Kennedy, but Johnson was an effective and supportive vice president. President Kennedy relied on Johnson and

> **O**n May 28, 1962, the New York Stock Exchange had its worst day since the Big Crash of 1929. It would be called Black Monday as stockholders lost nearly $21 billion. The market recovered by the next day.

Johnson was always closely identified with Texas, where he built his political career and honed his skills and rapport with the voters. *(Library of Congress)*

Johnson was so far ahead in the polls during the 1964 election, he did not need to campaign much. Here, he waves to supporters in Cleveland, Ohio. *(Lyndon Baines Johnson Library and Museum)*

his experience for advice on appointments, congressional strategy, and policy, both domestic and foreign. Johnson also traveled extensively for the administration, visiting 33 countries in three years. He often visited developing countries and used his own simple style of folksy diplomacy to promote the United States in the cold war. It was valuable experience for Johnson's presidential ambitions, and he would put it to use much sooner than anyone expected, after President Kennedy's assassination in November 1963.

REPLACING CAMELOT

President Johnson faced an enormous challenge as he was about to complete the final year of Kennedy's term. Kennedy's youth and charisma had made him very popular. As the 1960s had started, Americans were looking for leadership and direction, and Kennedy had provided that. A grieving United States did not see these same qualities in Johnson. He was older and lacked Kennedy's wit and style. It would be an uphill battle for him to gain the support of most Americans, and he did not have much time because 1964 was an election year.

Johnson did, however, have one tremendous skill—he was a master at getting legislation passed. To honor the fallen president and to gain the public's trust, he worked hard to get several of Kennedy's programs passed in Congress. The first was Kennedy's civil rights bill. He influenced Congress until he had enough votes to avoid a filibuster, the ploy southern senators had used in the past to kill civil rights bills. On July 2, 1964, Johnson signed the Civil Rights Act, which banned discrimination in public places and employment based on race, religion, and sex.

Johnson followed that victory with the passage of Kennedy's "war on poverty" plan. In August, he signed the Economic Opportunity Act, which provided nearly $1 billion for education, job training, and loans to small businesses, to help stop the cycle of children born into poverty without the means to make progress. Johnson also managed to get Kennedy's idea of a tax cut for the middle class passed. The $11.5 billion break added an extra $800 million per month to an already strong economy. Johnson concluded his respects to the former president by getting $5 billion from Congress for the space program.

THE GREAT SOCIETY

The strategy worked: The United States did not have Camelot back, but Americans saw that they had a president who cared and who could get things done. Johnson felt confident to start pushing his own plans, especially a domestic agenda that would go beyond Kennedy's New Frontier. The president called it the "Great Society," and it included the development of a wide range of domestic programs. Johnson wanted to end poverty and racial injustice. He proposed increased aid to education, the Job Corps, and a domestic Peace Corps called VISTA (Volunteers in Service to America). He wanted health care available to be available to more

President Johnson talks to a Job Corps student in Maryland. The Jobs Corps created training and jobs for school dropouts.
(Lyndon Baines Johnson Library and Museum)

In the first major college campus protest of the decade, 796 students were arrested at the University of California at Berkeley in December 1964. In this protest, a part of what they called the Free Speech Movement, the students took over the college administration building after the school chancellor tried to limit campus political activity.

Americans, especially the elderly, who had been hardest hit by the rising costs of health care. The Great Society also included employment programs, financial aid for the arts, and a reduction in pollution. It was the biggest welfare program since the New Deal, and Johnson had a huge Democratic majority in Congress to support him.

Johnson's first step in creating the Great Society was the creation of the Office of Economic Opportunity (OEO) in August 1964. The purpose of the agency was to manage the various programs of the war on poverty. The OEO immediately created several programs whose ultimate goal was to prevent poverty. Operation Headstart established preschools for children to improve education. The Jobs Corps created jobs for school dropouts. Upward Bound provided aid for needy students to attend college. The Neighborhood Youth Corps gave job training to unemployed teenagers. The Teacher Corps trained new teachers for improved education, particularly in poor areas.

The OEO also created VISTA, the program of volunteers who spent their two-year terms teaching vital skills to Americans in poor communities. Like the Peace Corps, VISTA programs emphasized health care, agriculture, and education. In the spirit of the times, VISTA workers also taught the poor how to organize and become more politically active. Workers and residents learned how to put pressure on local authorities to provide goods and services. This part of the program was controversial, and volunteers were told to stick to teaching skills, but for many of their students, the lessons had already been learned.

THE 1964 ELECTION

The 1964 presidential election turned into the largest popular vote landslide in U.S. history. The Republicans nominated Senator Barry Goldwater from Arizona who seemed to be the direct opposite of Johnson. He looked

upon Johnson's sweeping programs as creeping social-ism, in which the government has too much control over people's lives. He opposed the Civil Rights Act, and spoke of stronger military action to win the cold war, including Vietnam. Americans were in no mood to turn the clock back on racism or escalate a war, so Johnson won easily. Johnson looked upon his landslide election as a mandate from the people for the Great Society.

The first year of Johnson's term included more domestic victories. In 1965, Congress approved Johnson's new Department of Housing and Urban Development and allocated a huge $7.5 billion for housing subsidies for the poor. Congress also renewed the $1 billion war on poverty budget and approved an additional $1.3 billion in school aid for urban areas. Some Americans were concerned about Johnson's near-ly $100 billion budget to fund these programs, but the president argued that in the long run, the elimination

The Ku Klux Klan and an African American clash at the 1964 Republican Convention. The KKK's support for Barry Goldwater probably did not help the nominee. *(Library of Congress)*

"Extremism in the defense of liberty is no vice."

—Republican presidential candidate Barry Goldwater's campaign statement that cost him many votes in 1964

First Lady Lady Bird Johnson (center) campaigned for her husband during the 1964 campaign with a Whistle Stop tour aboard the Lady Bird Special train. *(Lyndon Baines Johnson Library and Museum)*

"To live anywhere in the world today and be against equality because of race or color is like living in Alaska and being against snow."

—U.S. writer William Faulkner

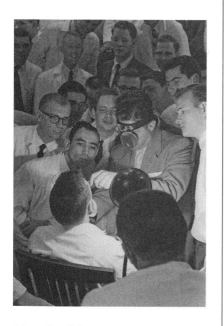

New health care programs for the poor and elderly increased the need for doctors. Above is a crowded classroom at George Washington University medical school. *(Library of Congress)*

of poverty and improved education returned much more than was spent.

One of the most important aspects of Johnson's Great Society was health care for more Americans. The idea had been discussed since the late 1940s, when President Harry Truman asked for a national health insurance program for all Americans. Because of the technological advances in medicine by the 1960s, such a program was far too costly, but Johnson still wanted health insurance for the neediest in the United States, the poor and the elderly. In August 1965, Congress approved two separate programs. Medicare was to provide health care for the elderly as an extension of Social Security, and Medicaid was to cover much of the poor's medical needs.

Johnson's Great Society was off to a tremendous start. The United States's affluence was being used to help all Americans. Johnson succeeded in getting 90 major bills passed in Congress in 1965 alone. There remained, however, two enormous problems, civil rights and Vietnam. Johnson's policies helped one of them, but the other would bring down both his presidency and the Great Society.

VOTING RIGHTS AND URBAN RIOTS

President Johnson was a strong supporter of the civil rights movement, and 1964 started out well for the cause. In February, the Twenty-Fourth Amendment to the Constitution eliminated the poll tax. The local tax had been used for years in the South as a means to prevent poor African Americans from voting. In early July, Congress passed the Civil Rights Act, which banned discrimination in employment, education, and public facilities. The summer of 1964 was also being called Freedom Summer by civil rights activists as hundreds of white students headed to Mississippi to work on African-American voter registration drives.

The summer in Mississippi, however, turned into a nightmare for the students and African Americans. The night the first group of volunteers arrived, six black churches were burned. On June 22, three volunteers, including two white students, were murdered by members of the Ku Klux Klan. Before the summer was over, there were three shootings and 80 beatings. Thirty-five

Andrew Goodman of New York City was killed near Philadelphia, Mississippi, while working for civil rights. *(AP/Wide World)*

The Civil Rights Act of 1964 ensured the voting rights of all Americans. Above, an African-American woman exercises her right to vote that year in Washington, D.C. *(Library of Congress)*

President Johnson often invited civil rights leaders to the White House. The 1964 meeting above included (left to right) Dr. Martin Luther King Jr., Whitney Young, and James Farmer. *(Lyndon Baines Johnson Library and Museum)*

Some African-American leaders had philosophical disagreements during the civil rights movement. Malcolm X spoke for many who grew impatient with nonviolence. *(Library of Congress)*

black churches were burned and 30 black homes were firebombed. The registration drives enlisted only 1,200 new black voters. More than 90 percent of Mississippi's eligible black voters remained unregistered.

Despite the gains being made in the civil rights movement and Martin Luther King Jr.'s pleas for non-violence, African-American communities were angry in the summer of 1964, especially in northern urban areas. Blacks were hearing many of their leaders reject nonviolence as a strategy. Malcolm X, a particularly influential militant activist, said, "An integrated cup of coffee does not pay for 400 years of slave labor." Many years of pent-up rage in black communities was ready to explode in the summer heat.

The violence started in New York City on July 18, when an off duty policeman shot and killed a 15-year-old black student who was having a dispute with a white apartment superintendent. Two nights later, a group of blacks went to the police precinct in Harlem to protest what the community was calling a murder. When they were denied access to the station, young blacks on the rooftops surrounding the building threw bottles, bricks and garbage at the police below. The first race riot of the summer of 1964 was on. For the next five nights, mobs of angry blacks roamed Harlem smashing windows and looting stores. The police tried to control the crowds by using nightsticks and arresting offenders, but the police were outnumbered. The riot then spread to the Bedford-Stuyvesant neighborhood in Brooklyn. Before the violence was over, there were two dead, 140 injured, over 500 arrested, and over 500 stores looted.

For the rest of the summer, violence spread to other black ghettos across the country, usually ignited by a single incident but fueled by years of frustration. Riots hit Rochester, New York; Jersey City, New Jersey; Philadelphia; and Chicago, with hundreds injured, thousands arrested, and entire neighborhoods destroyed. And there were more long hot summers to come in the 1960s.

In January 1965, King was asked to join a voter registration drive in Selma, Alabama. Civil rights workers had discovered that only about 300 of 15,000 eligible black voters were registered there. For years, local authorities had imposed special tests or taxes to prevent blacks from voting.

King organized many marches to the courthouse to register local blacks, but the activists were denied entrance each time. Some people trying to register were beaten or arrested. On February 1, 700 protesters, including King, were arrested. The following day, 500 schoolchildren demonstrated against King's arrest, and the local sheriff arrested them. As usual, the television cameras were there and Selma was getting national attention. President Johnson held a press conference to condemn the local authorities for preventing voter registration. Despite his comments, the situation got worse.

On February 19, one of the demonstrators, Jimmy Lee Jackson, was shot and killed by a state trooper as he carried his injured grandfather into a building. The death shocked the protesters into organizing a 58-mile march from Selma to Montgomery, the state capital. Their goal was to demand voters' rights from Governor

> **M**artin **L**uther **K**ing **J**r. won the Nobel Peace Prize in December 1964 for his nonviolent campaign against racial discrimination in the United States.

> *"It is a time for martyrs now and if I am to be one, it will be in the cause of brotherhood. That is the only thing that can save this country."*
>
> —Black leader Malcolm X in Selma, Alabama, three weeks before his assassination in 1965

"The vote is the most powerful instrument ever devised by man for breaking down injustice."

—President Johnson, upon signing the 1965 Voting Rights Act

The United States dropped more bombs on North Vietnam during the Vietnam War than it did on Germany and Japan combined in World War II.

George Wallace. Six hundred people showed up for the march in Selma, but state troopers, some on horseback, met the peaceful marchers at the bridge leading out of town and attacked them with clubs and tear gas. Americans again saw the violence on their televisions that night.

President Johnson called it "an American tragedy" and promised King's followers federal protection for another march. He also announced that he was sending a voting rights bill to Congress. On March 20, 1965, 4,000 marchers followed King out of Selma with members of the National Guard for protection. By the time they arrived in Montgomery five days later, there were 25,000 marchers. The march did not have much effect on Wallace, but on August 6, Johnson signed the Voting Rights Act, which banned local and state governments from using taxes, tests, and other unfair practices to restrict voter registration. Within a year, the number of blacks registered to vote rose from 29 percent to 52 percent.

Just five days later, however, a race riot erupted in the black ghetto of Watts in Los Angeles, after a white police officer pulled over a black driver who had been speeding. A crowd gathered to protest the officer's rough treatment of the black youth and the violence escalated. For the next six days, thousands of rioters looted stores, burned down entire blocks, and battled the police. Fifteen thousand National Guard troops finally restored order, but the cost was huge. There were 35 dead, 900 injured, 4,000 arrested, and $40 million in damage.

ESCALATION IN VIETNAM

Another battleground was also heating up in the summer of 1964. On August 2–3, two U.S. destroyers, the *Maddox* and the *C. Turner Joy* reported that they had been fired upon by North Vietnamese torpedo boats in the Gulf of Tonkin, located to the east of North Vietnam. The U.S.

President Johnson signs the Gulf of Tonkin resolution in the White House. The bill gave the president absolute power to escalate the Vietnam War as he saw fit. *(Lyndon Baines Johnson Library and Museum)*

Navy said their ships had been in international waters, but North Vietnam claimed they were within its waters.

In the United States, an important debate arose: How could the United States legally conduct a war in Vietnam if Congress had never declared war? President Johnson took advantage of the torpedo boat incident to ask Congress to pass the Gulf of Tonkin Resolution, giving him, as commander in chief, special executive privilege to conduct the war in Vietnam. The bill passed both houses nearly unanimously. It was the first step in a huge escalation in the Vietnam War.

In late 1964 and early 1965, Viet Cong attacks on U.S. military bases in Vietnam increased. One attack on the air base at Bien Hoa killed four U.S. soldiers and wounded another 72. An attack on Pleiku killed 32 more soldiers. As these attacks continued, Johnson ordered a series of air bombings of North Vietnam to destroy the North Vietnamese supply line from North to the Viet Cong in South Vietnam. The bombings included the use of napalm, a highly flammable chemical.

On November 2, 1965, Quaker Norman Morrison set himself on fire in front of the Pentagon in Washington, D.C., to protest the Vietnam War.

The bombings reflected the plan of the Johnson administration to win the war quickly and withdraw U.S. troops. Throughout 1965, Johnson sent more troops to Vietnam. In March, the total stood at about 30,000 troops. By July, Johnson increased it to 75,000 and ordered that the monthly number of men drafted into the military be doubled. By the end of the year, there were 175,000 U.S. troops in Vietnam. The war budget also increased from $500 million in 1964 to $2.2 billion in 1965.

As the war escalated in 1965, so did the antiwar protests. At first, there were teach-ins held on college campuses across the nation to educate students about the war. The first teach-in was at the University of Michigan in Ann Arbor in March, which attracted hundreds of teachers and thousands of students to an all-night vigil. The largest teach-in, attended by 35,000 students and teachers, was at the University of California at Berkeley, where the Free Speech Movement had started the year before. In April, Students for a Democratic Society (SDS) organized an antiwar demonstration at the White House, which drew 15,000 protesters. In October, 100,000 demonstrators in several U.S. cities, including 20,000 in Washington, D.C., protested the war.

Johnson tried to encourage peace negotiations at the end of the year, but North Vietnamese leader Ho Chi Minh insisted that the United States withdraw all its troops from Vietnam before there could be any negotiations. The U.S. death toll in Vietnam rose from 164 killed in 1964 to 1,340 dead in 1965.

TRIUMPHS IN SPACE

There were no manned space flights in 1964, but the unmanned *Ranger 7* lunar mission sent back over 4,000 photos of the moon before the spacecraft made its scheduled crash on the moon's surface. NASA was also busy preparing its new Gemini program. Its purpose

Gordon Cooper was the first astronaut to sleep in space, to use a television camera on a mission, and to control his craft during re-entry. *(NASA)*

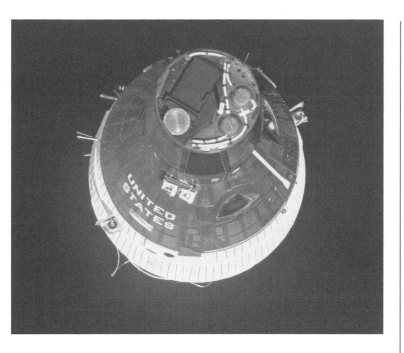

The Gemini space program lasted only 2½ years but included 12 missions. This is the view of *Gemini 7* taken from *Gemini 6* as the craft practiced maneuvers. *(NASA)*

was to develop the technology and functions needed for a manned lunar mission, including docking with another spacecraft, space walks, and precision landings.

In March 1965, *Gemini 3* became the first U.S. mission to send two astronauts into space together. The *Gemini 4* mission in June featured the first U.S. space walk. (The Soviet Union had their first space walk earlier in the year.) As astronaut James McDivitt piloted the *Gemini 4* spacecraft at around 17,500 mph, astronaut Edward White took a successful 22-minute walk in space while tethered to the spacecraft.

In July, NASA's *Mariner 4* unmanned mission flew within 6,000 miles of Mars and sent back photos of the planet's craters. In August, astronauts Gordon Cooper and Charles Conrad tested maneuvering techniques and equipment with their eight-day, 120-orbit *Gemini 5* mission.

The busy year concluded with two missions one week apart: *Gemini 6*, with astronauts Walter Schirra and Thomas Stafford, and *Gemini 7*, with astronauts James Lovell and Frank Borman. The two spacecraft

HISTORIC EARTHQUAKE ROCKS ALASKA

It was not just humankind that was restless in the 1960s. Mother nature shook the world with two of the largest earthquakes ever recorded. The largest measured 9.5 on the Richter scale and hit South America in May 1960, killing thousands. The other measured 9.2 and struck Alaska on March 27, 1964, killing 131 and causing more than $400 million in damage. (By comparison the quake that caused a tsunami in the Indian Ocean in December 2004 measured 9.0 and was the largest since 1964.)

The Alaska earthquake was twice as powerful as the one that destroyed San Francisco in 1906. The number of deaths was relatively low because of the small population of the area, but the town of Valdez was completely destroyed and thousands were left homeless. In Anchorage, Alaska's largest city, most of the office buildings were destroyed. The quake caused tidal waves called tsunamis.

The 1964 Alaska earthquake hit Seward, Alaska, particularly hard. A tsunami demolished the harbor and killed 11 people. *(National Oceanic and Atmospheric Administration)*

On the night of April 11, 1965, a series of violent tornadoes swept through several states in the Midwest, killing 253 people and causing $235 million in damages. The event came to be known as "the night of the twisters."

practiced docking techniques, coming within one foot of each other at one point. The *Gemini 7* mission also went on to set a space endurance record by staying in space for 14 days.

MUSIC IN THE 1960s

When Elvis Presley burst on the music scene in the mid-1950s, it seemed rock 'n' roll would become the dominant music on the U.S. scene. By the end of the 1950s, however, Presley was in the army and the industry was tarnished by the payola scandal. Over 250 disc jockeys, including the father of rock 'n' roll Alan Freed, were convicted of accepting cash or gifts to play certain songs. Rock 'n' roll remained in a decline through the early 1960s, but other styles of music rose in popularity and set the stage for a decade of music known for its variety and innovation. It was through music more than any other medium that young people expressed their feelings about life in the 1960s.

Folk music had enjoyed some popularity since the 1930s when Woody Guthrie sang socially conscious songs such as "This Land Is Your Land." Because folk music had a tradition as protest music, it fell out of favor in the 1950s when conformity was commonplace and dissent was frowned upon. As the 1960s evolved into a decade of protest, however, folk music experienced a revival.

At the head of the folk movement was folksinger Joan Baez, spokesperson for the new counterculture, who used her music as a political message. Baez consistently appeared at antiwar, antidraft, and civil rights demonstrations singing popular protest songs, such as "We Shall Overcome" and "Carry It On." She was often arrested for civil disobedience at these protests, along with other demonstrators. Baez was also at the center of the folk scene in New York City's Greenwich Village, where she met the singer and songwriter who would become one of the major voices of the 1960s, Bob Dylan.

Dylan, a huge fan of Woody Guthrie, came to New York in 1960 to visit the ailing singer. He joined the Greenwich Village scene and wrote many of the major protest songs of the early 1960s, such as "The Times They Are A-Changin'," "Blowin' in the Wind," and "A Hard Rain's A-Gonna Fall." Dylan stayed at the forefront of the folk movement until 1965, when he turned increasingly to rock and his lyrics became more personal and poetic. His new sound influenced many imitators and became known as folk rock—rock with a message.

Two musical styles kept rock 'n' roll afloat in the early 1960s: the African-American Motown sound and the white surfer groups. Songwriter and producer Berry Gordy formed the Motown record label in Detroit, Michigan, in 1959 to highlight black singers, particularly all-girl groups. Another brilliant record producer, Phil Spector, had many hits such as "Da Doo Ron Ron," and "Then He Kissed Me," by the Crystals and "Be My Baby," and "Do I Love You?,"by the Ronettes. Black groups also

"We are the antidote, the medicine man dispensing the balm for a very sick society."

—Beatles manager Brian Epstein on the reason for the group's tremendous popularity

Woody Guthrie (above) suffered from Huntington's chorea, a degenerative inherited disease of the nervous system. Despite Guthrie's illness, his meeting with Dylan in 1960 hugely influenced the younger singer. *(Library of Congress)*

The Barbie doll was so popular in 1965 that it made $97 million for the Mattel Toy Company.

AMERICAN BANDSTAND POPULARIZES ROCK

In the early 1960s, 20 million U.S. teens raced home from school everyday to watch *American Bandstand* on their televisions. Hosted by announcer Dick Clark, the show played teens' favorite rock 'n' roll songs and introduced them to new ones. The songs were often performed live (with lip-synching) by guest stars, such as Chubby Checker, Frankie Avalon, Fabian, or the Everly Brothers. As the songs played, teen couples performed the latest dance crazes. There were also dance contests, spotlight dances, and ratings of new songs.

The show was sometimes criticized for playing only the music of the most clean-cut rock 'n' roll stars rather than the songs of wilder stars, such as Elvis Presley and Hank Ballard. However, the show set another important standard—it was integrated and showed white and black teenagers together for the first time on a national program. It also offered many African-American singers and musicians their first national exposure. *American Bandstand* switched to a weekly format in 1963 but it continued to be broadcast with its ageless host Dick Clark until 1989.

> **T**he Beatles's first single, "I Want to Hold Your Hand," sold more than 1 million copies within 10 days of being released in the United States in 1964.

> *"I'd rather have 10 years of superhypermost than live to be 70 by sitting in some damn chair watching TV."*
>
> —Rock diva Janis Joplin, commenting on the "live now" philosophy of the 1960s

were successful with popular dance songs such as "The Watusi," "The Mashed Potatoes," and "The Twist."

The surfer music of Jan and Dean and the Beach Boys was a suburban fantasy, in which song lyrics idealized the party scene on California beaches with "two girls for every boy." Only one of the Beach Boys surfed, and most of their fans had never been to California, but such songs as "Surfin' Safari," "California Girls," and "Fun, Fun, Fun" in the early 1960s kept the party going until another superhero like Elvis came along to resurrect rock. That moment came in 1964.

When the Beatles, a British group, burst onto the U.S. music scene on "The Ed Sullivan Show" on February 9, 1964, more than 70 million people were watching. That broadcast launched a national passion or craze known as "Beatlemania." The Beatles sparked a period of tremendous creativity and variety in rock music, and the rest of the decade became rock's peak era. John Lennon, Paul McCartney, George Harrison, and Ringo Starr captured young women's hearts with their good looks and mop top long hair, but it was their distinctive sound that made them megastars. They borrowed the sounds of white and black early rock 'n' roll musicians such as Elvis, Chuck Berry, and Little Richard, and added their own simple lyrics and pleasing harmonies from Lennon and McCartney.

Beatlemania inspired a movement called the British Invasion. The most notable of these groups was the Rolling Stones, who cultivated a more urban, bad-boy image. As the decade progressed, rock music became more intricate, as it experimented with different sounds and more intense, socially conscious lyrics. Toward the end of the decade, rock musicians were disillusioned about their inability to change the world, and they turned to darker songs, including the Beatles's "A Day in the Life," and the Rolling Stones' "Sympathy for the Devil."

Blacks continued to make a huge contribution to the music of 1960s with the Motown sound and soul music. African-American Berry Gordy perfected a clean-cut look and sound that also appealed to white audiences. He dressed his Motown performers in evening clothes and glamorous wigs and created a unique style of choreography. He often backed their vocals with the Detroit Symphony, but he always made the songs easy

MASSIVE BLACKOUT AFFECTS MILLIONS

At 5:16 P.M. on November 9, 1965, a transmission line relay, about the size of a cigar box, failed at an electricity station in Ontario, Canada, and the city went dark. It may not sound like this mishap could cause much of a problem, but within minutes, 30 million people throughout Canada and the northeastern United States were without power. The problem was caused by electric generators that are linked over a wide area. When one breaks down, the others overload and break down. The breakdowns in 1965 quickly spread across the U.S.-Canadian border into New York State. By 5:28, New York City was dark and within 12 minutes, 80,000 square miles were affected.

In New York, the subways stopped in their tracks, stranding nearly 1 million commuters at rush hour. Thousands more were trapped in elevators. Traffic lights went out leaving drivers on their own at intersections. Some brave volunteers ventured into the intersections to direct traffic. Hospitals without their own generators delivered babies by candlelight. Two deaths were reported in New York, both on dark stairways, and the 320 prisoners at a state prison in Massachusetts took advantage of the darkness and attempted a mass escape. The tear gas guns still worked, and the riot was put down.

The blackout lasted about 13 hours in New York. Commuters fought over dark hotel rooms, many up long flights of stairs. Many people who could not get a room camped out in the train stations and airports. Governor Nelson Rockefeller also opened up the armories for those who could not get home. Telephones remained in service, and the phone company handled 14 times its usual load. According to the police, the crime rate did not rise. After the blackout was over, electric company executives investigated the incident and assured customers steps had been taken to prevent another blackout, but they happened again in the Northeast in 1977 and 2003.

"We're more popular than Jesus Christ right now."

—Beatle John Lennon's controversial statement on the popularity of his group

to dance to. The result was a string of hits from Smokey Robinson and the Miracles, the Temptations, the Supremes, the Four Tops, and other groups.

Soul music, on the other hand, appealed more to the heart as it combined the influence of blues and gospel music. Soul singers Otis Redding and James Brown gave energetic, emotional performances that were born in the struggle of the African-American experience. The Queen of Soul, Aretha Franklin, reached the top of the charts in 1967 with "Respect," a song written by Redding.

Another factor in the development of rock music in the 1960s was the use of LSD, a hallucinogenic drug also known as "acid." Its use inspired a form of music known as acid rock. Acid rock got its start in California with such groups as the Jefferson Airplane and the Byrds. The Jefferson Airplane's song "White Rabbit" and the Byrds's "Eight Miles High" are two popular examples of this form of rock music, also known as psychedelic rock. The Beatles also experimented with LSD for the *Sgt. Pepper's Lonely Hearts Club Band* album, considered by many rock critics to be the greatest rock album ever. The brilliant guitarist Jimi Hendrix and the blues-influenced singer Janis Joplin were two other rock stars who fully embraced drugs in their music and lives to "shut out the world," as Hendrix said.

CHAPTER 5

WAR PROTESTS AND RACE RIOTS, 1966–1967

THE ESCALATION OF THE WAR IN Vietnam continued throughout 1966 and 1967. The number of U.S. troops doubled in 1966 from 175,000 to 350,000, and by the end of 1967, there were 490,000 in Vietnam. The war also spread to new areas. There was now fighting in the neighboring nation of Cambodia because the North Vietnamese and the Viet Cong were using it as a refuge from U.S. military attack. For the first time the United States started bombing North Vietnam's capital of Hanoi and its nearby port of Haiphong to destroy military supplies, especially

President Johnson reviews the troops at Fort Campbell, Kentucky, in July 1966. American troop strength in Vietnam doubled in 1966, but the war remained a stalemate. *(Lyndon Baines Johnson Library and Museum)*

By 1967, the military told President Johnson that all "major military targets" in Vietnam had been destroyed. Battles like Dak To (above) continued, however. *(U.S. Army)*

"We had to destroy the town in order to save it."

—An army major in Vietnam after giving the orders to destroy the city of Ben Tre in South Vietnam because some Viet Cong had taken refuge in it

oil. Hanoi had been avoided as a target previously because its large civilian population. Haiphong had not been bombed because of the Soviet freighters delivering military aid.

Huge offensives were launched, combining American and South Vietnamese troops in areas of South Vietnam controlled by the Viet Cong. The Ho Chi Minh trail, which was used to deliver supplies and soldiers from North Vietnam into South Vietnam, was heavily bombed. There were constant assurances from President Johnson and his military commander in Vietnam, General William Westmoreland, that victory in the war was near. Johnson visited the troops personally in October 1966 to show his support and confidence.

It became clear to many Americans, however, that victory was a long way off, and the war had become a horrible stalemate. In 1966, Democratic senator J. William Fulbright held a Senate investigation of the U.S. policy in Vietnam, accusing the Johnson administration of lying to Americans about the war's progress. Many Americans followed the Senate hearings on television and became concerned. They had also seen graphic coverage of the war on television and were wondering why a superpower like the United States could not easily defeat a small, undeveloped nation like North Vietnam.

Arkansas's Senator Fulbright was chairman of the Senate Committee on Foreign Relations that investigated the Johnson administration's handling of the Vietnam War. *(Lyndon Baines Johnson Library and Museum)*

No one was more troubled by Vietnam than Johnson, whose dreams of a Great Society were dying because of the war. Despite the huge U.S. effort to win the war, it had become a stalemate for several reasons. The Soviet Union was supplying North Vietnam with the most advanced military supplies, including antiaircraft weapons, which shot down 335 U.S. planes in 1966 alone. Another reason for the slow progress was the desertion rate in the South Vietnamese army. In 1966, there were 100,000 deserters, some of whom joined the Viet Cong.

As World War I had shown earlier in the century, a stalemate can lead to high death rates, as was the case in Vietnam. Because the Johnson administration saw a North Vietnamese–Viet Cong death rate 10 times higher than the U.S.–South Vietnamese rate, they assumed victory was near. U.S. leaders did not realize that the North was prepared to sacrifice vast numbers of troops for their cause.

The U.S. death count was 6,500 in 1966 and 9,300 in 1967, bringing the total for the war to more than 16,000. The financial cost of the war also took its toll. In September 1967, the Johnson defense budget was a record $70 billion, $20 billion of which was for Vietnam. However, the Great Society was not yet dead in 1967. The federal budget called for another $1.8 billion for the

"Hey, hey, LBJ, how many kids did you kill today?"

—A favorite chant of antiwar protesters during President Johnson's escalation of the Vietnam War

South Vietnam's president Nguyen Van Thieu (above) once served with North Vietnam's leader Ho Chi Minh. The two split when Ho Chi Minh became a communist. *(Lyndon Baines Johnson Library and Museum)*

On June 13, 1966, the Supreme Court ruled in *Miranda v. Arizona* that all criminal suspects must be advised of their civil rights at the time of their arrest, including the right to remain silent.

war on poverty, but it was not the struggle that was getting all the attention.

WAR PROTESTS SPREAD

After President Johnson doubled the draft in mid-1966, many young people were alarmed that they would be forced to serve in a war that most of them strongly opposed. As antiwar protests increased, the director of the Selective Service, Lewis Hershey, ordered all local draft boards to reclassify all arrested protesters as 1-A; that is, to be placed in the top rank of those to be called up for military service. He also decided that student deferments, or postponements, from the draft would be limited and based on academic performance. In June 1967, Johnson extended the draft for four years and canceled all deferments for graduate students.

As a result of these developments, antidraft protests increased, and some young men publicly burned their draft cards. Antiwar and antidraft groups often protested together and organized break-ins at draft registration centers to destroy draft records. Many young men opposing the draft fled to Canada to avoid service in Vietnam. It is estimated that nearly 70,000 Americans moved to Canada during the 1960s to avoid the draft.

Antiwar protests continued to grow, and they no longer included only students. On March 25–27, 1966, protests were held in several cities, including New York, where 25,000 demonstrators showed up. In May 1966, 10,000 protesters picketed the White House in full view of Johnson. On April 15, 1967, 125,000 people participated in the largest antiwar demonstration to date in New York. Another huge protest in San Francisco had 75,000 demonstrators.

For the most part, these protests were peaceful, with speeches, music, posters, and buttons voicing the new

antiwar slogans. The most common were "Make Love, Not War" and "Flower Power." A popular visual was the U.S. flag with a peace sign drawn over it. Protesters also adapted the hand symbol of the first and middle fingers raised in a "V" to show their support for peace.

The first violence at an antiwar protest occurred at the October 1967 march on the Pentagon. After 100,000 protesters gathered at the Lincoln Memorial, about half of the group marched two miles to the Pentagon, the central headquarters of the U.S. military. Their intent was to encircle the building and gain entry. With bayonets drawn, 6,000 soldiers and 2,000 members of the National Guard met the demonstrators. As some of the protesters placed flowers inside the soldiers' guns, others tried to force their way into the Pentagon. They were beaten back with nightsticks and tear gas, resulting in 47 injuries and 650 arrests.

One new supporter of the antiwar protests and draft resistance was civil rights leader Martin Luther King Jr. King appreciated Johnson's strong support of civil rights, but he felt the war and draft were wrong for two reasons. First, he believed the huge amounts of

Vietnam War protestors march on the Pentagon in October 1967. Many veterans of the war took part in this march. *(Lyndon Baines Johnson Library and Museum)*

In May 1967, Vietnam War and draft protesters assembled outside the gates of the White House. Included in the group is Coretta Scott King, wife of Dr. Martin Luther King Jr. *(Lyndon Baines Johnson Library and Museum)*

The March on the Pentagon protest in October 1967 turned violent when protestors tried to enter the military complex.
(Lyndon Baines Johnson Library and Museum)

In 1967, the Supreme Court ruled that laws in southern states forbidding marriages between blacks and whites were unconstitutional.

money spent on the Vietnam War could be put to better use at home to fight the war on poverty. He also realized that a disproportionate number of soldiers in Vietnam were black, because they were too poor to be in college and have access to student deferments. Many young black men joined the military as their only way to make a living. King condemned the war as racist and encouraged draft resistance by both black and white young people.

RACE RIOTS AND BLACK POWER

In June 1966, civil rights activist James Meredith organized a 250-mile voter registration march through Tennessee and Mississippi. The march was the beginning of a deep split within the movement. Meredith had not marched very far when he was shot and injured by a white racist. Leaders from several civil rights groups, including Stokely Carmichael from the Student Nonviolent Coordinating Committee (SNCC) and King from the SLCC, decided to complete the march for Meredith.

Along the way, Carmichael was arrested for trying to set up some tents for the night. When he was released the next day, he chanted the slogan, "Black Power." This act caused a split in the civil rights movement.

The Black Power movement was born in October 1966 with the formation of the Black Panther Party in California by black activists Huey Newton and Bobby Seale. The purpose of the Black Panthers was to encourage African Americans to defend themselves and to call for a reorganization of U.S. society to make it more equal. The new movement was militant and rejected King's nonviolence. It called on blacks to use violence when necessary for self-defense.

As the long hot summer of 1966 approached, riots seemed inevitable. The first broke out in July in Chicago. King was in Chicago supporting his new civil rights plan in which the northern urban areas would become open cities. King realized that poverty, even more than segregation, was a key element underlying the problems of northern blacks. His open city idea led him to ask Mayor Richard Daley for better schools, more jobs, and a minimum wage. King also called for integrated housing projects rather than black housing projects, which kept the city segregated.

Mayor Daley was not receptive and the city's blacks grew frustrated. Once again, a small event triggered an explosion of anger. When the police turned off a fire hydrant that was cooling off some African-American children, the community exploded. Groups of blacks rampaged their neighborhoods looted stores. This time it was gunfire that came down on policemen from the rooftops, not bricks. It seemed that some blacks had been listening to the new Black Power

H. Rap Brown's leadership of SNCC ended in 1970 when legal problems forced him into hiding. The group that had started with the sit-in movement in 1960 became defunct. (*Library of Congress*)

On January 13, 1966, Robert Weaver became the first African-American member of the president's cabinet when President Johnson appointed him head of the new Department of Housing and Urban Development.

ORGANIZING THE MIGRANT WORKERS

In the early 1960s, conditions for migrant workers on California farms were terrible. Most migrant workers were badly paid Mexican Americans. Even though child labor was illegal, children worked with their parents and families and were exposed to dangerous pesticides. In 1962, Cesar Chavez, an ex-migrant worker, who was helping the workers find housing and medical care, decided to unionize the farm workers.

Chavez called the union the Farm Workers Association and went from farm to farm over hundreds of square miles recruiting workers. By late 1965, the workers had a large union, but the farmers did not recognize it. The workers went on strike for better wages, safer working conditions, and recognition of their union. They gained the support of a national labor union, the AFL-CIO, and became the United Farm Workers union, but some grape farmers still refused to negotiate with them. The strike grew into the largest farm worker strike in California history.

Chavez followed the lead of Martin Luther King Jr. and the civil rights movement, insisting on nonviolence from his members. He organized a boycott with the help of college students and civil rights groups and asked people across the United States not to buy California grapes raised with nonunion labor. During the boycott, he also went on a hunger strike, refusing to eat for 25 days in 1968. The boycott and Chavez's leadership gained the support of Americans. Eventually the grape growers recognized the union and met their demands.

Eldridge Cleaver was Minister of Information for the Black Panther party. His 1968 book, *Soul on Ice,* became a best-seller. *(Library of Congress)*

philosophy. The next night, 4,000 whites rioted. King had rocks and a knife hurled at him. Four thousand National Guard troops were called in to restore order.

Sixteen more cities erupted during the summer of 1966, but the following year was much worse. Even before that summer began, black students rioted at a Nashville college after a Black Power speech by Carmichael. Throughout the summer, H. Rap Brown, the new leader of the SNCC, toured black ghettos and encouraged followers to "burn this town down."

In June, Boston, Buffalo, Atlanta, and Cincinnati erupted. In July, a Black Power convention in Newark, New Jersey, called for armed rebellion against white racism and the creation of two nations, one white and one black. Several days of rioting followed causing 26 deaths and 1,500 injuries. That same month, Detroit erupted in the worst race riot of the summer, leaving 43 dead, 300 injured, and $300 million in property damage. In all, there were 75 riots in 1967, in which 83 people lost their lives, 2,000 were injured, and 12,000 arrested.

Robert Kennedy, senator of New York, called it the greatest domestic crisis since the Civil War. President

Johnson appointed the U.S. National Advisory Commission on Civil Disorders to investigate the riots. One year later, the commission put the blame on widespread, institutionalized white racism throughout the entire nation and recommended an expansion of many of Johnson's Great Society programs before it was too late.

WOMEN'S RIGHTS: FRIEDAN AND NOW

The women's rights movement began in 1848 with the Seneca Falls Convention in New York State, demanding equal rights with men on issues such as voting, access to higher education and jobs, land ownership, and custody of children. Progress was very slow over the next century, and women did not even gain the right to vote until 1920. Other gains, such as equal pay for equal work, came much more slowly. Despite this fact, more and more women entered the workforce, reaching a peak during World War II when they were needed in defense plants because men were fighting the war overseas.

After the war, returning veterans took back the women's jobs, and the baby boom started. Most women again became primarily homemakers and mothers. Television shows during the 1950s reinforced the idea of a woman's place being in the home, but many women felt unfulfilled by this limited role. Events in the 1960s eventually led to a revival of the women's rights movement.

The first event was the Food and Drug Administration's (FDA) approval in 1960 of the female contraceptive pill to prevent pregnancy. It came to be known as "the pill," and it gave women the freedom to choose when and if to have babies. Freed of constant childbearing, many women chose to seek careers outside the home and pursued a different identity and role in society.

Some women chose political activism to advance causes they supported. In November 1961, 50,000 U.S.

Thurgood Marshall served as Chief Counsel for the NAACP from 1939 to 1961. *(Library of Congress)*

In 1967, Thurgood Marshall became the first African American appointed to the U.S. Supreme Court.

women participated in demonstrations across the country in an organization called Women Strike for Peace. The demonstrators demanded that the Kennedy administration end the nuclear weapons buildup of the cold war and consider equal rights for women. Kennedy directed Congress to create the Commission on the Status of Women to study the issue, and on June 10, 1963, Congress passed the Equal Pay Act, promising women equal pay for equal work. It was a start, but the law only affected the few jobs that both men and women performed. Without education and training, working women were still stuck in low-paying jobs, such as teaching, nursing, and secretarial work. In 1963, the average female worker's salary was less than 60 percent of the average male's.

Also in 1963, Betty Friedan gave the women's movement a boost with her book *The Feminine Mystique*. The book gave a voice to women who were feeling that their lives lacked meaning because they kept house and raised children. Friedan called their dilemma "the problem that has no name." She mainly blamed the government and the media, both dominated by males, for the problem. Friedan said the government held women back by not ensuring their equal access to education and jobs. She said the media, such as television, magazines, and advertising, wanted to keep women in their traditional role so that they would continue to buy products for the home. Friedan's book sold more than 2 million copies, and women's rights was back in the news.

Friedan also helped found the National Organization of Women (NOW) in 1966 to fight for women's rights. By the end of the decade, NOW had over 8,000 members. It called for better child care programs to allow mothers to pursue careers and job training, abortion rights to end unwanted pregnancies, and the addition of an Equal Rights Amendment (ERA) to the Constitution to guarantee equality of the sexes.

Writer Betty Friedan became one of the leaders of the women's movement in the 1960s after the publication of her very popular *The Feminine Mystique. (Library of Congress)*

In March 1967, Senator Eugene McCarthy introduced a proposal to Congress for an equal rights amendment. It passed Congress, but needed the approval of 38 state legislatures to become law. (To date, the ERA has not been ratified by the necessary number of states.)

NOW also helped women learn political activism. At first, their involvement was combined with the civil rights and antiwar movements, but by the end of the decade, they started organizing their own events. In March 1969, Women Strike for Peace demonstrated in Washington, D.C., against the Vietnam War. Also in 1969, writer Gloria Steinem wrote a magazine article, "After Black Power, Women's Liberation." Women's liberation would become one of the major movements of the 1970s.

Both Gloria Steinem (shown here) and Betty Friedan were Smith College graduates. They also both helped found the National Women's Political Caucus in 1971. *(Library of Congress)*

A TRAGEDY IN THE SPACE PROGRAM

The year 1966 was the busiest and most expensive in NASA's history, costing nearly $8 billion. In an effort to win the race to the moon, there were five manned missions completing the Gemini program. Each of the flights continued to work on activities required in a lunar mission. The two most important tasks were the spacecraft docking maneuvers, which were required for the two-craft moon landing, and the space walks, to see if astronauts could work in the weightlessness of space. On the *Gemini 8* mission, astronauts Neil Armstrong and David Scott accomplished the United States's first successful docking maneuver as their spacecraft linked up with an unmanned target vehicle. In *Gemini 12*, astronaut Edwin Aldrin took three separate walks, including a two-hour space walk, the longest ever taken.

NASA always had to balance the political pressure on the race to the moon with safety. The speedy completion of the Gemini program put the United States clearly ahead of the Soviet Union, but several problems arose during the missions. The biggest scare happened

The Apollo space program had a tragic start when the crew of the first mission—Ed White, Gus Grissom, and Roger Chaffee (left to right)—died in a capsule fire during training. *(NASA)*

In January 1967, the United States and the Soviet Union signed a treaty restricting the use of outer space for military purposes. The treaty also prohibited claiming ownership of the moon and planets.

"If we die, we want people to accept it. The conquest of space is worth the risk of life."

—Astronaut Gus Grissom, who later died along with two other astronauts in the fire aboard the *Apollo 1* spacecraft

on *Gemini 8* when a short circuit made the spacecraft shake so violently that the mission was immediately returned to Earth. The *Gemini 9* mission failed on its docking attempt, and a space walk was cut short due to a problem with the life support system. *Gemini 10* and *Gemini 11* also had to limit their space walks because of equipment problems.

NASA's Apollo program was scheduled to accomplish a lunar landing well before the end of the decade. On January 27, 1967, the *Apollo 1* crew, Virgil 'Gus" Grissom, Ed White, and Roger Chaffee, were in training for a February mission when disaster struck. During a practice launch, a flash fire broke out in their spacecraft killing all three astronauts. An investigation revealed several problems in the design of the spacecraft. It would be nearly two years before NASA attempted another manned mission.

THE COUNTERCULTURE: HIPPIES AND DRUGS

In the 20th-century United States, it was common for the youth of each generation to go through a period of rebellion before they matured into adulthood. In the

POP ART: ANYTHING GOES

In the 1960s, art began more and more to reflect the youth counterculture and its desire for alternatives to the conventional. Some artists began creating art for a much wider audience than just wealthy collectors. To appeal to this TV-generation audience, artists used images from popular culture, especially advertising, for their subjects. They called their work pop art and the leaders of the movement included Andy Warhol and Roy Lichtenstein among others.

Warhol became famous as much for his wild Greenwich Village parties as for his bold prints showing Campbell's Soup cans and Coca-Cola bottles. He also created posters of celebrity faces, including Marilyn Monroe. Lichtenstein painted oversize panels of comic strip paintings complete with dialogue and sound effects. The respectability of pop artists grew among others in 1963 when the Guggenheim Museum in New York City sponsored a major pop art exhibit.

"In the future, everybody will be famous for 15 minutes."

—Pop artist Andy Warhol on the mass media's effect on fame

1920s, some young people went to speakeasies and drank illegal alcohol. In the 1940s, they embraced the energetic beat and dances of swing music. In the 1950s, rock 'n' roll gave teens a rebellious identity. The rebellion of the youth of the 1960s, however, seemed more extreme because their society was suffering from so many threatening problems.

From the time the young people of the 1960s were children, they had heard about nuclear war and had witnessed the world brought close to destruction by the Cuban missile crisis in 1962. Teens and young men faced having to serve in a horrible war halfway around the world in the jungles of Vietnam. Riots hit scores of U.S. cities as African Americans reacted violently to years of racism and poverty. Pollution was contaminating the earth's air and water. The country that their parents' generation had fought so hard to save did not seem to live up to its ideals.

Because young people believed that so many things had gone wrong in the world, they felt that many things had to be changed. Like most generations, they developed their own fashions and music, but the changes they made went much deeper. In a nation of

Hippie style was even adopted by the wife of a young Marine P.O.W. *(National Archives)*

HAPPENINGS AND BE-INS

A distinctly 1960s cultural event was called a happening. Happenings were part art exhibit, part theater, part music, and were always unpredictable. They took place in specially created settings that were decorated with unusual objects and psychedelic designs, and they included performers acting spontaneously. The audiences were often encouraged to participate in any way they wanted. The subjects of happenings could be anything from fast food to a car crash.

Performance art grew out of the happening phenomenon. The idea of performance art was to create a live piece of art in which both the performer and the audience became a part of the work. For instance, one performance artist, Yoko Ono (who later married Beatle member John Lennon) staged a performance in which the audience cut away pieces of her clothing while she knelt silently.

The event called a be-in was a result of the growing interest in Eastern (Asian) philosophy and religions, which emphasized the importance of "being" as opposed to the Western ideal of "doing." The largest be-in took place in San Francisco's Golden Gate Park on January 14, 1967, and was called "Gathering of the Tribes." Twenty thousand participants attended and listened to rock music from the Jefferson Airplane and the Grateful Dead. They also heard Allen Ginsberg read his poetry and LSD guru Timothy Leary tell them to "tune in, turn on, and drop out." Many experienced LSD-induced hallucinations from the free doses of the drug passed among the crowd.

conformity, violence, and intolerance, they tried to create a culture of individuality, peace, and understanding. Many young people decided to retreat from the nation's overwhelming problems and make a new society. It was called the counterculture and many of those involved in it were called hippies.

The beginnings of hippie culture appeared in 1965, when young people seeking an escape from what they called "the establishment" flocked to the Haight Ashbury section of San Francisco. They wore colorful new clothes with beads and flowers, listened to rock music, and had a freer attitude toward sex. Many hippies were also heavy drug users, particularly of LSD and marijuana, both of which provided escape.

One of the reasons California became popular with the first hippies was that LSD was still legal there in the mid-1960s. The drug had become well-known through the work of Harvard psychologist Timothy Leary who claimed it expanded consciousness. LSD is a powerful drug that produces numerous hours of vivid, colorful hallucinations. Sometimes, the experience is referred to as a "good trip" because the world seems much more

The term *hippie* probably came from the word *hip,* an early 1960s reference to a drug user.

beautiful under the drug's influence. Other times, the drug causes a "bad trip" and the world appears threatening. Hallucinations can often return to users even when they are not using the drug, and it can lead to dangerous behavior. By the end of 1966, LSD was made illegal throughout the United States.

Marijuana was popular with the Beat generation in the 1950s, and many hippies embraced it as their favorite drug. It was illegal in the 1960s but was readily available. Marijuana is a milder drug than LSD and produces a dream-like state in which the senses often seem stimulated. Its major effect is a contented passivity, in which the problems of the real world seem unimportant. One of the causes that the counterculture fought for was the legalization of marijuana. (More recent studies of marijuana have not supported legalization of the drug due to its long-term side effects. They indicate that marijuana use can lead to respiratory ailments similar to those caused by cigarette smoking and can cause permanent brain impairment.)

The hippies of Haight Ashbury reached their high point with the "Summer of Love" in 1967. During that summer, young people came to the area by the thousands and found an oasis of peace amidst all the violence in the country. Trying hard to live up to their ideals, hippies shared everything they had, especially their drugs. The highlight of the summer was the Monterey Pop Festival, when 50,000 young people showed up to see several of their favorite rock groups play. Its success led to other music festivals including Woodstock in New York in 1969.

By the end of 1967, it was apparent that the hippie community at Haight Ashbury was falling apart. Tour buses and television cameras roamed the neighborhood to gawk at the hippies. LSD had become illegal, and crime was on the rise as drug dealers and drug addicts took over the streets. In October 1967 the hippies held a Death of Hip funeral in Golden Gate Park

Jimi Hendrix was among the performers at the Monterey Pop Festival. (Photofest)

LOOKING OUT FOR THE CONSUMER

During the 1950s, the president of General Motors said that what was good for General Motors was good for the country. Big business boomed during the postwar 1950s and 1960s, but was it at the expense of the consumer? Attorney and consumer rights activist Ralph Nader thought so, and in a decade of civil rights, he became the leader of the consumer rights movement. His first target was General Motors. In 1965, Nader published *Unsafe at Any Speed,* a book blasting the car industry for placing profits ahead of safety.

In his research, Nader singled out the sporty Corvair, manufactured by General Motors, as a particularly hazardous vehicle. The Corvair was very popular in the early 1960s, but it also suffered from a high accident rate. Nader said the car's rear engine design and suspension system were causing accidents, and he called it, "One of the greatest acts of industrial irresponsibility in the present century." General Motors tried to discredit Nader, but when it reported a record $2.1 billion profit for 1965, Americans were on Nader's side. Corvair sales dropped sharply and production of the car stopped four years later. Nader's work led to the passage of the National Traffic and Motor Vehicle Safety Act in 1966, which gave the federal government control over automobile design and safety.

Nader hired a staff of consumer rights activists, called Nader's Raiders, and they investigated other industries risking the public's safety. His investigation of meat processing plants prompted Congress to pass the Wholesome Meat Act of 1967, which required regular federal inspections of plants. Nader has continued to be active and has taken on other safety issues, such as pollution, nuclear plant dangers, and medical health hazards. In the process, he has turned many Americans into smarter consumers.

with a fake corpse holding a flower. They set the coffin on fire and left Haight Ashbury. Some hippies disappeared into groups called communes and moved to more isolated areas to live closer to nature and survive on their own. Some went to college and others joined the various protest movements. The term *hippie* eventually came to mean almost any young person who dressed differently.

TELEVISION

There were two sides to television in the 1960s. In one way, it was often hard to tell from the programming that the 1950s were over. The same types of shows—westerns, sitcoms about white families, and variety programs—still dominated. Among the westerns were the long-running *Gunsmoke* (1955–75), *Bonanza* (1959–73), and *Wagon Train* (1957–65). Popular sitcoms included *The Dick Van Dyke Show* (1961–66), *The Beverly Hillbillies* (1962–71), and *The Adventures of Ozzie and Harriet* (1952–66). The most popular variety shows were among the longest-running shows in television history—*The Ed Sullivan Show* (1948–71), *The Lawrence Welk Show* (1955–82), and *The Tonight Show* with comedian Johnny Carson (1962–92).

Television had little reason to change because it was more popular than ever. In 1960, 45 million families owned a television. By the end of the decade, that number had risen to 60 million. Only a few shows reflected the changes that were going on in U.S. society. The boldest was *The Smothers Brothers Comedy Hour* (1967–69). The show started out as a regular variety show, but by 1968, comedians Tom and Dick Smothers were booking controversial acts and taking a stand against the Vietnam War. Guests included folk singer Pete Seeger, who sang the antiwar song "Waist Deep in the Big Muddy." It was Seeger's first television appearance since being blacklisted by the McCarthy hearings in the 1950s. Joan Baez appeared and spoke about her husband who had been jailed for resisting the draft. The show also had a regular character, the "hippie chick," who bragged of her drug experiences. Because the show was controversial, CBS network executives canceled it midseason.

Rowan and Martin's *Laugh-In* (1968–73) was a different, fast-paced comedy show that carefully attempted some social satire. Its emphasis was on laughs rather than social and political statements, so it enjoyed a five-year run. The science fiction series *Star Trek* (1966–69) made several statements about race relations and pollution, but it was somewhat protected from controversy because the story took place in the future. When the sitcom *Julia* premiered in 1968, television finally had a series dealing with a black family. The adventure series *I Spy* (1965–68) also featured a black costar in Bill Cosby. Other than that, blacks rarely saw black performers when they watched television.

Television news programs brought reality home in the 1960s. Every night with news anchors Walter

The Department of the Interior issued its first endangered species list on March 1, 1967. The list contained 78 species, including the bald eagle and the grizzly bear.

The term *bald* in *bald eagle* actually means "marked with white." (*U.S. Fish and Wildlife Service*)

By the 1960s, TV news cameras, like this one at a student demonstration, were everywhere, catching news as it happened. Americans were better informed and could make up their own minds on the decade's vital issues.
(Lyndon Baines Johnson Library and Museum)

Cronkite of CBS, and Chet Huntley and David Brinkley of NBC, Americans saw graphic pictures of the Vietnam War, urban riots, student demonstrations, and political assassinations. Bloody scenes of Americans dying in Vietnam were seen repeatedly on television during the 1960s and played a large part in fueling the antiwar movement. By the end of the decade, television was the main provider of both entertainment and information for Americans. It was also playing a key role in forming public opinion.

Walter Cronkite presented the disturbing coverage of the Vietnam War in an intelligent and calm manner, earning the trust of millions of Americans.
(Library of Congress)

CHAPTER 6

ASSASSINATIONS AND CRISIS, 1968

THE MOST CRITICAL YEAR OF THE decade in the Vietnam War was 1968. The year started out on a promising note when North Vietnamese leaders said peace talks could begin if the United States put a halt to bombing. Previously, they had insisted that all U.S. troops leave the country before talks could begin. President Johnson's administration thought they might have finally gained the upper hand. The previous year ended with a lull in the fighting, and Johnson wondered if North Vietnam might finally be weakening. He hated that the war had

President Johnson's visit to the troops in Vietnam was not enough to turn the tide in the war. The communist Tet Offensive in 1968 proved that the war could not be won. *(Lyndon Baines Johnson Library and Museum)*

After years of promising that victory in Vietnam was near, General Westmoreland was relieved of duties as commander of the armed forces in April 1968. *(Lyndon Baines Johnson Library and Museum)*

distracted him and Americans from his plans for the Great Society, but he refused to withdraw troops from Vietnam and be the first U.S. president to lose a war. General Westmoreland assured him that there was a "light at the end of the tunnel."

Just the opposite was true. On January 30, the communists launched a surprise attack of 80,000 North Vietnamese and Viet Cong troops throughout the south. They even assaulted the U.S. embassy in Saigon. In the first two weeks of the offensive, over 1,100 U.S. lives were lost. On February 1, American television audiences saw the brutal execution of a suspected Viet Cong soldier by South Vietnam's national police chief on the streets of Saigon.

In March, a counteroffensive of 50,000 U.S. and South Vietnamese troops drove the communists back, but the damage had been done. Almost all Americans now knew the United States was far from winning the war. After so many years and deaths, it was still a deadly stalemate. U.S. soldiers also sensed the futility of the war and some acted on their frustration. Many turned to drugs, which were readily available in

THE JUNGLE WAR

Although the United States had fought in the tropical South Pacific in World War II, it had never undertaken a war in a country like Vietnam. The environment consisted of dense jungles and flooded rice paddies that made fighting very difficult. The weather was usually extremely hot and wet. Soldiers also had to contend with blood-sucking leeches that had to be burned off the skin. The North Vietnamese knew they could not equal the U.S. soldier's weaponry so they devised other tactics.

The communists booby-trapped the jungle with trip wires that set off bombs when soldiers came in contact with them. They also made hidden pits filled with poison-tipped bamboo stakes and spears that were automatically set to be thrown when the slightest pressure landed on a vine or a root. Both sides buried mines throughout the jungles, their locations known only to the opposing army. Hundreds of hidden tunnels allowed the Viet Cong and North Vietnamese troops to ambush U.S. soldiers and disappear quickly again.

An even bigger problem for the U.S. soldier in the Vietnam War was the Viet Cong within South Vietnam. The Viet Cong soldiers did not wear uniforms and looked exactly like South Vietnamese residents. American soldiers could not tell who was an enemy and who was an ally. The confusion caused the deaths of many innocent victims. Sometimes entire villages of families were wiped out as the stress of the unusual war grew.

Vice President Hubert Humphrey and First Lady Lady Bird Johnson actively aided Johnson in reaching out to voters and potential voters. Here they ride in an antique automobile during a country fair. *(Lyndon Baines Johnson Library and Museum)*

In August 1968, Abby Hoffman, Timothy Leary, and Jerry Rubin (left to right) announced their plans to disrupt the Democratic National Convention in Chicago. *(AP/Wide World)*

Vietnam. Desertions rose and few soldiers turned to fragging, killing their officers to avoid being sent into battle again. The worst violation came when a company under the command of army lieutenant William Calley massacred 370 civilians, including women and children, while on a search for Viet Cong in the town of My Lai.

By April 1968, President Johnson was devastated. He announced he would not run again for the presidency in the upcoming election and said he would try to find a way to end the war. The U.S. troop count in Vietnam was at its highest, totaling 543,000. General Westmoreland was replaced as commander of the forces in Vietnam. Peace talks between the North Vietnamese and the United States began in Paris in May, but they dragged on for several years. The war continued for the rest of Johnson's term, but the troop count never rose again. By the end of the year, the total number of U.S. deaths from the war climbed over 30,000.

YIPPIES AND THE CHICAGO POLICE

Antiwar protests continued throughout 1968, including huge demonstrations overseas in Japan and France. At

"I shall not seek and will not accept the nomination of my party for another term as your president."

—President Johnson's surprise television announcement, in which he declined to run again for the presidency

As part of a national trend away from capital punishment, 1968 marked the first year since 1930 that there were no executions in the United States.

In the 1967 congressional elections, Shirley Chisholm became the first female African-American member of the U.S. House of Representatives.

home, college campuses remained the center of activity. The largest protest was at Columbia University in New York City where 1,000 students took over several campus buildings to oppose the war and the school's ties to some Pentagon research on campus. Over 700 students were arrested before it was over. Students at the University of California at Berkeley, the University of San Francisco, and the University of Wisconsin also demonstrated, and there was a "National Turn in Your Draft Card Day," but years of protests had not ended the war and students had grown frustrated and cynical.

The frustration led to a more militant approach by some radical groups, including the SDS and the Yippies (Youth International Party), and they organized a protest for the Democratic National Convention in Chicago in August. These groups had come to believe that creating confrontation with the police was a more effective tactic to get their antiwar message across. They were joined by the usual nonviolent demonstrators and, by the time the convention started, 10,000 protesters had gathered in Chicago's Grant Park.

Chicago's Mayor Richard Daley was prepared with 12,000 police, 5,000 National Guard troops, and 6,000 army reinforcements. On the night of the Democratic Party's nomination of Vice President Hubert Humphrey, a Vietnam War supporter, thousands of protestors tried to march from Chicago's Grant Park to the amphitheatre where the convention was taking place. The police, in full riot gear with clubs, tear gas, and mace, blocked the demonstrators and there was a brief standoff. As some of the protestors taunted the police, tension grew until the police suddenly attacked the protestors, including some reporters and bystanders who got in the way. A crime commission that later investigated the event called it a "police riot" and concluded the police had committed violent acts far in excess of what was necessary.

During the riot, many protestors started chanting, "The whole world is watching," and they were right.

THE FBI SPIES ON "ENEMIES"

The FBI had a long history of fighting crime by the 1960s. Many young people looked upon FBI agents, or G-men, as heroes. In the 1960s, however, FBI director J. Edgar Hoover chose some unlikely people to investigate as enemies of the United States. One was Martin Luther King Jr. Hoover became obsessed with the civil rights leader and was convinced that King was under communist direction to destroy the country.

Hoover ordered secret wiretaps of King's phones wherever he went and sent agents as spies to join the civil rights movement and report on the civil rights leader's activities. The FBI deliberately spread false rumors about King being involved with white women outside of his marriage. Because of Hoover's obsession, there

Critics of J. Edgar Hoover believe he abused his powers as director of the FBI to conduct a personal vendetta against Dr. Martin Luther King Jr. *(Lyndon Baines Johnson Library and Museum)*

were suspicions that Hoover and the FBI might have been involved in King's assassination. There were lingering doubts that a drifter like James Earl Ray could have acted alone, largely because of the amount of money Ray needed to stalk King for weeks before the killing and to fund his escape to England afterward.

At the very least, the FBI showed little interest in protecting King from the numerous death threats the black leader received over the years. Years later, in a 1979 congressional hearing on assassinations, an Atlanta FBI agent testified that under Hoover's direction, "we were operating an intensive vendetta against King in an effort to destroy him." After Hoover's death in 1972, the FBI underwent enormous changes, as ordered by Congress.

Television cameras caught the event live and millions of Americans as well as delegates inside the convention hall watched in disbelief as the violence in the streets of Chicago unfolded. A debate developed among the delegates inside the convention as antiwar supporters blasted Mayor Daley who sat in the front row with the Chicago delegates. As Humphrey gave his acceptance speech, the sound of police sirens and screaming crowds could be heard in the background. After it was all over, 1,000 protestors were injured and 600 arrested.

THE ASSASSINATION OF MARTIN LUTHER KING JR.

The rise of African-American groups urging violence and the 1967 riots in black communities were very troubling to Martin Luther King Jr. He had faith in the

"How many men must die before we can really have a free and true and peaceful society? How long will it take?"

—Coretta Scott King, after the assassination of her husband Martin Luther King Jr.

The Poor People's March on Washington in May 1968 was planned by Dr. Martin Luther King Jr. It took place, however, one month after his assassination in Memphis. *(Library of Congress)*

morality and effectiveness of nonviolence, and he could point to the passages of the Civil Rights Act and the Voting Rights Act as proof. As the riots continued, he thought of stepping aside and letting the violence run its course, believing it would eventually fail.

Instead he started a new antipoverty movement. King knew overcoming poverty was the next important step for African Americans, but he also realized it affected all Americans and was likely to inspire wider support than the civil rights movement. To highlight his new Poor People's Campaign, King planned a massive Poor People's March to take place in Washington, D.C., in May 1968. King hoped the march would raise public support as successfully as the March on Washington had in 1963. As he was completing preparations for the march, King was asked to go to Memphis, Tennessee, to support striking sanitation workers. On April 4, as King stood on his hotel balcony, he was assassinated by James Earl Ray, a white drifter and convict

For the next week, enraged and grieving black communities across the United States erupted in the worst violence the country had seen since the Civil War. Riots broke out in 168 cities, with Washington, D.C., Baltimore, Chicago, and Kansas City being the worst hit. When it was all over, there were 46 dead, over 2,000 injured, 24,000 arrests, and over $50 million in damages. While the riots were raging, 150,000 people attended King's funeral in Atlanta, Georgia. His coffin was carried through the streets on a simple farm wagon drawn by two mules, a symbol of King's compassion for the poor and oppressed.

One week after the assassination, Congress passed the Civil Rights Act of 1968, which prohibited discrimination in housing. It was now illegal to refuse to sell or rent housing to anyone based on race. The Poor People's March also took place as planned under the leadership of the new leader of the SCLC, civil rights leader Ralph Abernathy. A shantytown called Resurrection City was built near the Lincoln Memorial, and hundreds lived in it for several weeks as a reminder to Washington's rich and powerful elite. On June 19, over 50,000 demonstrators marched from the Washington Monument to the Lincoln Memorial and heard speeches by supporters of the movement, including Coretta Scott King, the slain civil rights leader's widow.

THE GREAT SOCIETY: A DREAM DIES

When President Johnson was preparing for his 1968 State of the Union address, he told his speechwriter to make no mention of the Great Society. The president's dream had died. Johnson's conflict during his presidency was referred to as "guns and butter." The *guns*

Reverend Ralph Abernathy led the Poor People's March on Washington after King's assassination. Speakers at the demonstration included Coretta Scott King, the slain leader's widow. *(Library of Congress)*

A 1969 poster calls for a "Don't Work" day to honor Dr. King on the anniversary of his death. His birthday was made a national holiday by Congress in 1983. *(Library of Congress)*

Washington, D.C., was one of the cities hardest hit by the 1968 race riots after Dr. Martin Luther King Jr.'s murder. National Guard soldiers had to be called out to restore the peace. Such scenes helped Lyndon Johnson gain congressional approval for increased funding for urban areas. *(Library of Congress)*

referred to the Vietnam War and the effort to stop the spread of communism. The *butter* referred to the domestic programs and his war on poverty. Johnson thought he could have both, but the huge expense of the war forced him to choose. Because the demands of the cold war were still strong in the 1960s, he chose guns.

Despite this choice, Johnson proposed increased spending on urban housing and employment in his final budget. The unemployment rate was at its lowest in 15 years, and the poverty rate was nearly cut in half during his presidency. Civil rights and Medicare were also lasting achievements of the Great Society, but these accomplishments were just the beginning of what Johnson had intended to achieve.

In one of the year's few bright spots, NASA's Apollo program made a big comeback from its tragedy the year

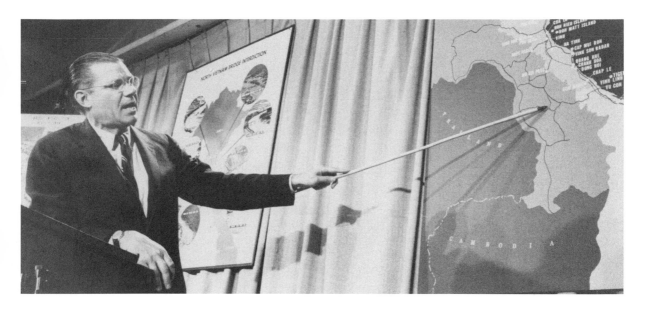

before. NASA spent over $400 million in safety improvements to the Apollo spacecraft, and *Apollo 7* in October 1968 was the first successful manned mission in 21 months. *Apollo 8's* astronauts Frank Borman, Jim Lovell, and William Anders took the final step toward a lunar landing with the first manned moon orbit. After getting as close as 70 miles above the lunar surface and completing 10 orbits, *Apollo 8* made the 200,000 mile return trip safely. NASA was almost ready for a lunar landing.

THE 1968 ELECTION

As the campaign for the 1968 presidential election began, it seemed there were clear front-runners for each party. Richard Nixon had worked hard for Republican candidates in the 1966 election and was lining up strong support within the party. President Johnson had his problem with the Vietnam War, but he had a strong domestic record and little competition. In the first primary in New Hampshire, only the little known Senator Eugene McCarthy of Minnesota opposed the president with his antiwar message, but he had little money to spend on a campaign.

Secretary of Defense Robert McNamara was one of the strategists of the Vietnam War. His eventual disapproval of the war led to his resignation in 1968. *(Library of Congress)*

Richard Nixon's nomination for the 1968 presidential election was a stunning comeback. Just six years earlier, he had told reporters, "You won't have Nixon to kick around anymore." *(Library of Congress)*

Senator Robert Kennedy became the front-runner for the Democratic nomination after President Johnson withdrew from the race. *(Library of Congress)*

"Some men see things as they are and say why. I dream things that never were and say why not."

—Senator Robert Kennedy, during his campaign for the presidency

College students worked hard for McCarthy in New Hampshire, and when the votes were counted on March 12, Johnson won by a small margin of 48 percent to 42 percent. Johnson and the rest of the Democratic Party were stunned. Four days after the New Hampshire primary, Senator Robert Kennedy entered the race, as another antiwar candidate. Two weeks after that, a war-weary President Johnson shocked the country by withdrawing from the race.

The Democratic nomination was now up for grabs and on April 26, Vice President Hubert Humphrey threw his hat into the ring. As the three candidates battled each other in a series of primaries, it seemed Senator Kennedy was the front-runner. He was the antiwar candidate who had the most money to run a strong campaign, and he received support from voters who wanted to recapture the excitement and hopefulness of his brother's years in the White House.

On June 5, Kennedy won the last and crucial primary in California to strengthen his lead. After his victory speech at his Los Angeles headquarters, however, he was assassinated by a young Jordanian, Sirhan Sirhan, who was furious at Kennedy's strong support for Israel in the Middle East. For the second time in barely two months, Americans were stunned and grieving the loss of another one of their leaders.

The Republican convention in Miami was quiet as Nixon won the nomination easily. He said he had a plan to end the war in Vietnam with honor, although he would not go into any details of the plan. With Kennedy's death, Vice President Humphrey was able to win the Democratic nomination in Chicago while protestors and police battled on the streets outside the convention hall. Humphrey had little choice but to run on Johnson's record.

To make the election even more complex, Governor George Wallace of Alabama decided to run as the candidate of a third party, the American Independent Party.

PROGRESS BRINGS POLLUTION

With NASA and the military receiving so much funding during the 1960s, there was a technology boom in the United States. There were tremendous advances in medicine, communications, and computer electronics, including the development of microchips, which would revolutionize computers. Advances in industry, however, meant an increase in the pollution of the nation's air, soil, and water.

Automobiles emitted carbon monoxide, a poisonous gas, and other hazardous substances that cause an increase in lung disease. (Cars still put these toxins into the air but in lesser amounts.) Industrial plants are often located along rivers and lakes where they dumped their waste products, including mercury, into the water killing fish and plants. Most sewage treatment plants dumped raw sewage into U.S. waterways. Emissions from the smokestacks of power plants and other manufacturers fell back to Earth, often in the form of acid rain, to contaminate the soil. An oil spill from an offshore oil rig in the Pacific Ocean was 10 miles long and threatened the coastline of California.

Congress started the fight against pollution with the passage of three bills in the 1960s—the Water Quality Act of 1965, the Wilderness Act of 1964, and the Air Quality Act of 1967. By the late 1960s, health food

Emitted as gases by the smokestacks (such as those shown) of power plants that burn fossil fuels, sulfur dioxide and nitrogen oxide are the primary causes of acid rain. *(Library of Congress)*

stores were appearing, selling organic foods that were grown without the use of pesticides. Recycling centers were also set up for newspapers and bottles. The environmental movement truly emerged on April 22, 1970, when the first Earth Day was organized to call attention to increasing destruction of Earth's resources.

His message was that Washington had grown too powerful and the concerns of regular Americans were being ignored. He vowed to restore law and order to the nation's streets. Some southern voters may have believed that he would try to restore segregation to the South.

The popular vote in the election was one of the closest ever, with Nixon beating Humphrey by only 500,000 votes nationwide. Nixon won the electoral vote easily, 301–191. Wallace made a strong showing for a third party candidate, carrying five southern states and collecting 10 million votes. As 1969 began, many Americans were eager to see President Nixon's plan to end the Vietnam War with honor.

"If this nation can afford to spend $30 billion to put a man on the moon, it can afford what it takes to put a man on his feet here on Earth."

—Vice President Hubert Humphrey in support of the Great Society's war on poverty

In 1968, 1.6 million students registered for college, a 50 percent increase since 1963. One reason was the improved education of Great Society programs; another was a desire for a student deferment to avoid the draft.

"It seems now more certain than ever that the bloody experience in Vietnam is to end in stalemate. The rational way out will be to negotiate, not as victors, but as honorable people who lived up to their pledge to defend democracy and did the best they could."

—CBS news anchor Walter Cronkite, in 1968 on the Vietnam War

THE AMERICAN INDIAN MOVEMENT

In the history of Native Americans, the decades of the 1950s and 1960s were known as the "termination period." In 1953, Congress voted to withdraw all federal support and responsibility for American Indian affairs. It was an attempt to treat Native Americans exactly the same as all other U.S. citizens, but the result was a disaster. By the late 1960s, millions of acres of Native American land had been sold, and thousands of Native Americans had become totally dependent on government welfare.

In 1968, a group of American Indians from Minneapolis, Minnesota, formed the American Indian Movement (AIM) in response to complaints about police brutality. The group monitored police behavior and, within a year, arrests of American Indians had decreased by 50 percent. The group also developed "survival schools," in which Native American children could learn about their culture. As a result of this early success, local chapters of AIM were formed, and by 1972, there were 40 chapters throughout the country.

In 1969, AIM members took part in the Native American occupation of Alcatraz Island in San Francisco Bay to draw attention to the plight of American Indians throughout the country. One of the demands of the group was to turn the island's abandoned federal prison into an Indian educational and cultural center. The occupation of the island lasted 19 months until 1971 when the protesters were forced off the island without any of their demands being met.

FASHION

The essence of the 1960s was nonconformity. It was a decade of rejecting the old and embracing the new. The need to explore alternatives grew into an obsession. Even the small details of fashion and appearance

Miniskirts were tremendously popular with young women. The length was always short, but styles varied from high fashion to the everyday comfort of simple cotton sundresses, like those shown here. *(Sunbird Photos by Don Byrd)*

became political statements. In many cases, the new look started simply with long hair, especially for men. At the time, long hair was a symbol of defiance and the easiest way to distinguish oneself from the older generation. The trend also gave rise to a hugely successful Broadway play, *Hair*, which was the first Broadway musical with a rock score. It ran for 1,750 performances.

New styles of clothing, such as the mod look (short for modern), appeared during the decade as many young people sought to express their individuality through fashion. One of the basics of the mod look was the miniskirt, first popularized in London by designer Mary Quant. Many women and girls wore miniskirts, sometimes imported from Great Britain, that fell several inches or more above the knee. Psychedelic or geometric designs and bright colors were popular, and beads replaced traditional jewelry. Go-go boots, usually white, or color coordinated tights were sometimes worn with the miniskirt. (The boots got their name from go-go bars, which featured dancers wearing the high boots dancing in hanging cages.)

After years of hearing the chant "Elvis Is Dead" from his fans, Elvis Presley performed on an hour-long television concert on December 3, 1968. The show was a huge success as Presley showed he still had the moves and the voice that made him a rock 'n' roll legend.

"Clothes are just not that important. They're not status symbols any longer. They're for fun."

— Fashion designer Rudi Gernreich, on 1960s clothing styles

The underground comics movement started in 1968 with the work of R. (Robert) Crumb's Zap Comix. The new comics dealt with adult issues (drugs, sex, and urban reality) rather than fantasy superheroes.

Male fashion in the 1960s also changed in a style often called the peacock revolution. It was an attempt to give men more options in the way they dressed. New male styles included textured vests and paisley shirts. Ties became wider and more colorful. Nehru jackets, named after Indian leader Jawaharlal Nehru (1889–1964), became popular. The Nehru jacket featured a stand-up collar instead of wide lapels, was made of lightweight material, and was often light-colored. For men who were less adventurous, a turtle-neck replaced the shirt and tie for a more informal look.

Many young people approached fashion with a desire to simplify. The hippie style differed considerably from the mod look as young people adopted the uniform of the decade, blue jeans and a t-shirt. The more devoted hippies also chose to simplify, but with more color and more organic shapes and designs. Hippie women often wore long, colorful "granny dresses," sometimes found in thrift shops. Both men and women wore the mark of the hippie, the tie-dyed shirt. Tie-dying is an ancient process practiced in China and Africa in which a piece of fabric or clothing item is knotted and dipped in several different dyes creating splotches of coloring. The shirts were often homemade and became the ultimate expression of individuality because each one was unique.

MOVIES

In the 1960s, the movie industry had one goal: It had to make money. The growing popularity of television was cutting into movie attendance and profits. One reaction in the industry was to make movies that dealt with subjects television avoided, such as sex, drugs, and violence. The graphic depiction of these subjects in the films of the early 1960s outraged conservative members of the public and led to a movie rating system. In 1966, the Motion Picture Association of America instituted the codes that indicated a movie's rating. "G" meant that a movie was intended for viewers of all ages and "PG" (originally "M" for mature audiences) indicated that parental guidance was advised. "R" meant that young people under age 17 must have a parent or guardian accompany them and "X" meant that no one under age 17 was to be admitted to a movie. The code made it easier for filmmakers to create the movies they wanted and easier for parents and other viewers to know what to expect in the movies they chose to see.

Hollywood in the 1960s was still dominated by familiar themes. There were musicals such as *The Sound of Music,* epics such as *Lawrence of Arabia,* and thrillers such as *Psycho,* but other films directly reflected the times. In the early 1960s, several films effectively dealt with the cold war and the nuclear threat. In fact, 1964 saw the release of three such films.

Stanley Kubrick's *Dr. Strangelove, or How I Learned to Stop Worrying and Love the Bomb,* dealt comically with the nuclear world as a mad general decides to drop a nuclear bomb on the Soviet Union because he fears the communists are trying to poison "our precious bodily fluids." In John Frankenheimer's *Seven Days in May,* a U.S. general plans to take over the government because he thinks the president is being too soft on the Soviet Union. In Sidney Lumet's *Fail Safe,* the United States's sophisticated defense system accidentally sends a plane loaded with nuclear weapons to bomb Moscow. Since the pilots are trained never to turn back after they have reached their "fail safe" point, Moscow is destroyed. The only way the U.S. president can avoid full-scale nuclear war is to destroy New York City with another U.S. nuclear bomb.

Two films in particular concerned young people rejecting the culture of their parents finding their own place in the world. In *The Graduate* (1967), directed by Mike Nichols, a recent college graduate, Ben, comes home to an upper-middle-class, suburban family who

On June 3, 1968, pop artist Andy Warhol was shot and seriously injured by a deranged woman who said she belonged to a movement called the Society for Cutting Up Men (SCUM).

In January 1968, a U.S. Navy spy ship, the *Pueblo,* was seized by North Korea and its 83 crewmen taken prisoner. The United States said the boat was in international waters, but it took nearly a year to negotiate the crew's release.

A young woman at an antiwar demonstration offers a flower to a military policeman. Flowers became a symbol of peace to the 1960s subculture. *(National Archives)*

thinks they know exactly what he should do. One family friend whispers in his ear, "I've got one word for you—plastics." Ben is lost and horrified at the prospect of following in his father's footsteps. He is seduced by a middle-aged friend of his parents and then finds himself in an awkward situation when he falls in love with her daughter. The film ends with the two young people running off together to an uncertain future.

The theme of *Easy Rider* (1969), directed by Peter Fonda (who also starred in it), was more countercultural. Two drug-using hippies ride their motorcycles from California to New Orleans in search of America and themselves. Along the way, they pick up a disillusioned lawyer, played by the young actor Jack Nicholson, and the three find little except drugs and sex. The film was a huge success among young people because it deals with the idealism of their search and the cynicism toward what they found. Although the characters' quest ends in disaster, because of *Easy Rider,* Kerouac's *On the Road,* and other novels and movies, thousands of young people took off on similar cross-country journeys in search of America.

"A man went looking for America and couldn't find it anywhere."

—An ad for the movie *Easy Rider*

CHAPTER 7

MAN WALKS ON MOON, STUMBLES ON EARTH, 1969

RICHARD MILHOUS NIXON WAS BORN on January 9, 1913, in Yorba Linda, California. He attended public schools in Whittier, California, and graduated from Whittier College in 1934. Nixon received his law degree from Duke University in 1937 and returned to Whittier to join a law office. Like Presidents Eisenhower, Kennedy, and Johnson before him, Nixon served in World War II. From 1942 to 1946, he served as a naval lieutenant in the South Pacific.

Nixon's political rise after the war was rapid. He was asked by California Republicans to run for a seat in the House of Representatives in 1946. During the

On July 16, 1969, *Apollo 11* astronauts Neil Armstrong and Buzz Aldrin spent 2½ hours on the lunar surface. They collected rocks, conducted experiments, and left behind an American flag. *(NASA)*

President Nixon delivers his inauguration speech from the portico of the U.S. Capitol. *(Library of Congress)*

Pat Nixon accompanied her husband, Richard, throughout his campaigns and on his many trips abroad as vice president. *(Library of Congress)*

campaign, he made a strong stand against communism and won the election easily in the new cold war atmosphere. In his first term, Nixon became a member of the House Committee on Un-American Activities, which was investigating communism in the federal government. He gained a national reputation for his investigation of Alger Hiss, a high-ranking official in the State Department. Hiss denied that he was involved in a communist spy ring, but he was convicted of perjury and sentenced to five years in prison.

After two terms in the House, Nixon ran for the Senate in 1950 against California member of Congress Helen Gahagan Douglas. He won easily by accusing his opponent of being "soft" on communism. Just two years later, presidential candidate Dwight D. Eisenhower chose Nixon to be his running mate in the 1952 election. This time Nixon accused the Democratic presidential candidate Adlai Stevenson of being lax in dealing with communism, and the Eisenhower-Nixon team won the election in a landslide. At age 40, he was the second youngest vice president in U.S. history.

The Eisenhower-Nixon ticket won another landslide in the election of 1956, and Eisenhower gave Nixon an active role in foreign policy during their two terms. Nixon traveled the world as a goodwill ambassador, presenting the U.S. position on the cold war conflict. In 1958, Nixon's limousine was attacked by anti-U.S. demonstrators in Caracas, Venezuela. They ripped off the car's U.S. flag, shattered the windows with rocks, and tried to overturn the car. Nixon barely escaped and was acclaimed a hero upon his return. In a 1959 visit to the Soviet Union, the vice president was in a televised debate with Premier Khrushchev about the benefits of U.S. capitalism over Soviet communism. He again strengthened his reputation as a strong leader defending his country's honor.

After eight years as vice president, Nixon was his party's obvious choice to run in the 1960 presidential election. He seemed to be leading against his Democratic opponent, Senator John F. Kennedy of Massachusetts, until a series of television debates toward the end of the campaign. Nixon seemed nervous and uncomfortable in front of the cameras whereas Kennedy spoke directly to them and the millions of voters watching at home. On Election Day, out of 69 million votes cast, Nixon lost by only 112,000 votes, what was at that time the closest election in presidential history.

Nixon planned another run for the presidency in 1964. He ran for governor of California in 1962, hoping that it would be the base for his campaign, but he also lost that election. At a press conference the day after the election, Nixon made a bitter farewell speech to the press and said he was finished with politics. In 1966, however, he campaigned hard for many Republican candidates throughout the country and set himself up again as the strongest Republican candidate for the 1968 presidential election. He took advantage of a deeply divided Democratic Party and won a close election.

INHERITING A NATION IN CRISIS

When President Nixon took office in January 1969, he was confronted with a nation in crisis. The civil rights movement had turned violent, and, since the death of Martin Luther King Jr. in 1968, it did not seem to have a national leader. Large antiwar protests filled the streets, and college campuses exploded into violence as students protested a variety of issues. To make matters worse, it was now apparent that the U.S. economy was suffering. The cost of living was at its highest rate in 20 years, and the balance of trade surplus was at its lowest point in 30 years. Unemployment and inflation were both rising sharply. The Vietnam War continued to be the country's most pressing problem. It was seriously affecting the nation's economy. The Tet Offensive in 1968 had made the war appear to be an unwinnable disaster, but the new president said he had a plan.

"Just think of how much you are going to be missing. You won't have Nixon to kick around anymore because, gentlemen, this is my last press conference."

—Former Vice President Richard Nixon, after losing the election for governor of California in 1962

Students for a Democratic Society sponsored conferences on campuses throughout the country. This leaflet announces a night of protest speakers at Michigan State University.
(Michigan State University Library)

Prince Sihanouk was leader of Cambodia during most of the Vietnam War. He kept his country neutral even though both communist and American forces violated Cambodian territory. *(Michigan State University Library)*

"Under no circumstances will I be affected by it."

—President Nixon, commenting on what he thought of the 750,000 protesters in Washington for the Vietnam Moratorium in 1969

VIETNAMIZATION

It was not until March that Nixon's secretary of defense Melvin Laird announced the president's plan to end the United States's involvement in the war. Called "Vietnamization," the plan involved the replacement of 543,000 U.S. troops by South Vietnamese forces. The timetable was vague, but Nixon said the number of U.S. forces would be reduced to 40,000–50,000 by the end of his first term.

A plan that called for at least four more years of military involvement in Vietnam was not acceptable to most of the U.S. antiwar protesters. Nor was another part of Nixon's strategy—a massive increase in the bombing of North Vietnam, including the use of 130,000 tons of explosives a month. The third part of the plan was secret. The CIA led a mission called Operation Phoenix to eliminate the Viet Cong from South Vietnam. Over the next four years, Operation Phoenix would kill at least 20,000 Vietnamese who were suspected of being Viet Cong or Viet Cong supporters. Even though U.S. troops were to be slowly withdrawn, Nixon was also trying to win the war. Like Johnson, he did not want to be the first U.S. president to lose a war.

The first 25,000 U.S. troops left Vietnam in June and, by the end of 1969, around 100,000 soldiers had come home, but the war raged on. Much of the fighting centered around Saigon, the South Vietnamese capital, to keep it from falling. Secretly, the U.S. military started bombing North Vietnamese base camps in Cambodia, from which they had been launching attacks on U.S. troops for years. In early 1970, Nixon announced that troops would enter Cambodia, but the air strikes remained secret for four years. During that time, 100,000 Cambodians were killed and 2 million were left homeless. The disruption of Cambodian life led to one of the bloodiest civil wars of the 20th century.

Meanwhile, the Paris peace talks went nowhere; it took weeks to reach an agreement on the shape of the table for the negotiations. Before the end of the year, the war had become the fourth deadliest in the nation's history after World War II, World War I, and the Civil War. As the decade ended, 40,000 Americans had died in the war, and despite Vietnamization, the end was not in sight.

DAYS OF RAGE

When President Nixon's Vietnam policy became clear, student protests grew angrier and the demands increased. Some members of the SDS split off into a pro-violence group called the Weathermen whose goal was to bring down the government in what they called "Days of Rage." That slogan described the entire year on college campuses throughout the country as war protests multiplied and students wanted to have more say in the administration of their schools.

Throughout the spring, the National Guard was called out to break up demonstrations at the University of Wisconsin, Duke University, and once again, the University of California at Berkeley. In April, 200 Harvard University students were arrested in a protest to have the U.S. military's Reserve Officers Training Program (ROTC) removed from campus, a common demand in student protests. In May, armed students took over campus administration buildings and destroyed the student center at the City College of New York. In all, 69 campuses in 23 states had demonstrations large enough to include arrests in 1969. The most tragic campus demonstration occurred the following year in May 1970 at Kent State University in Ohio. National Guard soldiers opened fire on students protesting the war, killing four and wounding eight others.

The biggest protest of 1969 turned out to be the largest demonstration ever held in Washington, D.C. On November 15, 750,000 people showed up to call for an end to the war. It was called Vietnam Moratorium

In order to make draft selection more fair, the Selective Service System started a draft lottery system in 1969, in which all draft registrants were randomly chosen according to a number assigned to their birth date.

"No matter where you travel, It's nice to get home. "

—Astronaut Neil Armstrong, after returning from his *Apollo 11* lunar landing mission

THE CHICAGO EIGHT

As the 1960s were ending, the political protesters of the counterculture were breaking up into separate groups. The protest movement had been too slow for some groups, including the Black Panthers who increasingly advocated violence. Students for a Democratic Society (SDS) split into two groups when their more radical, militant members formed the Weathermen. The Youth International Party, or Yippies, believed in combining protest with theater to dramatize the issues. They used humor and satire to show their disdain for the American government and try to bring about change.

In September 1969, a group of eight protesters from these groups were charged with conspiracy, inciting a riot, and other violent acts that occurred at the 1968 Democratic convention in Chicago. They were called the Chicago Eight and included Abbie Hoffman and Jerry Rubin from the Yippies, Tom Hayden and Rennie Davis from SDS, Bobby Seale from the Black Panthers, peace activist David Dellinger, and war protestors John Froines, and Lee Weiner. The trial came to symbolize the deep divisions in the United States between the counterculture and the establishment.

The judge for the trial was 73-year-old Julius Hoffman, who immediately showed a strong prejudice against the eight defendants. When Seale voiced his outrage at the judge's attitude, he was shackled to his chair and gagged. Judge Hoffman eventually banished Seale from the courtroom to be tried at a different time, but the battles between the defendants and their lawyers and Judge Hoffman continued. At one point, defendants Rubin and Hoffman showed up in judges' robes and said they loved being on trial because it was "good theater." There were several convictions in the trial, but they were all eventually overturned due to Judge Hoffman's unethical decisions.

(meaning suspension or strike) and was preceded by a 40-hour March against Death around the White House. The march consisted of around 40,000 people, each carrying a card with the name of a U.S. casualty in the Vietnam War.

"Man's destiny on Earth is not divisible...however far we reach into the cosmos, our destiny lies not in the stars but on Earth itself, in our own hands, in our own hearts."

—President Nixon reflecting on humankind's future after viewing U.S. astronauts landing on the moon

"ONE GIANT LEAP FOR MANKIND "

The 1960s was the decade President Kennedy had hoped to shape. As the decade came to an end, most of his hopeful vision had not come true. The cold war had become a real war in Southeast Asia. As a result, young people opposed their government rather than worked for it. Legal victories in the civil rights movement were overshadowed by violence in the streets across the United States. One of Kennedy's dreams was achieved, however—the United States landed a person on the moon.

In early 1969, there were two more preparation missions. Both the *Apollo 9* and *Apollo 10* spacecrafts consisted of two parts: the lunar module, which would separate from the spacecraft and fly to the moon and back, and the command module, which would orbit the moon and retrieve the lunar module. In *Apollo 9,* astronauts Jim McDivitt and Russell Schweickert undocked, or separated, the lunar module from the command module and flew independently for six hours, roaming up to 100 miles from the command module. *Apollo 10* again tested the capability of the lunar module, this time while in lunar orbit. Astronauts Thomas Stafford and Eugene Cernan flew the lunar lander within nine miles of the moon's surface before returning to the spacecraft.

On July 16, astronauts Neil Armstrong, Edwin "Buzz" Aldrin, and Michael Collins took off from Cape Kennedy in *Apollo 11,* the lunar landing mission. On July 20, Armstrong and Aldrin guided the lunar lander, the *Eagle,* to its landing spot on the moon's surface located in the Sea of Tranquility. Armstrong had to veer off course when he noticed rocks and boulders beneath him, but at 4:18 P.M. EST, he told mission control, "The *Eagle* has landed." They had only 15 seconds of fuel left.

At 10:56 P.M. EST that night, while an estimated 600 million people watched on television, Armstrong climbed down from the lunar lander and became the first person to step on the moon. His famous first words from the surface were, "That's one small step for man, one giant leap for mankind." Aldrin would join him later, and the two astronauts spent two hours on the surface completing several experiments, the most important of which was the collection of lunar soil and rocks to study back on Earth.

Before leaving, the astronauts also left behind a U.S. flag and a plaque inscribed, "Here men from planet Earth first set foot upon the Moon, July 1969, A.D. We came in peace for all mankind." They also sent back pictures of a beautiful blue and white Earth, which had a profound effect on many viewers. Many people wondered how turmoil and violence could be so common in such a peaceful-looking, beautiful world.

The first lunar landing mission, *Apollo 11,* lifts off from Cape Kennedy on July 16, 1969. It was President Kennedy who had challenged NASA to attempt such a mission eight years earlier. *(NASA)*

NASA scientists developed many items for the space program that later became popular products for the public, including Tang orange drink and Velcro fasteners.

President Nixon greets the *Apollo 11* astronauts after their return to Earth, as they wait in a decontamination chamber. *(NASA)*

New York City honored the *Apollo 11* astronauts with one of its largest ticker tape parades ever. None of the three men ever returned to space. *(NASA)*

The next day Armstrong and Aldrin blasted off from the moon and re-docked with the command module to join Collins for the long ride home. They all returned to Earth safely. Later, they had a heroes' welcome and a huge ticker tape parade in New York City. It was a sign of the times that some Americans condemned the mission as a waste of valuable money and resources when there were so many still suffering on Earth, but most people viewed it as an example of the wonderful things humans are capable of when they try.

WOODSTOCK: DEFINING A GENERATION

There was one more event in 1969 that helped the turbulent 1960s end on a proud note: the Woodstock Music and Art Festival in Bethel, New York, held August 15–17. Even more than drugs or protest, music was the focal point of the decade's counterculture. There were many young people who did not use drugs, and there were some who were not interested in protest, but there were very few who were not devoted to their generation's music.

The success of the Monterey Pop Festival during the 1967 Summer of Love resulted in several other large outdoor concerts, including one in Miami that drew 40,000 spectators. The organizers of Woodstock were able to book over 20 of the biggest names in rock for "Three Days of Peace and Music." The planners knew it was going to draw at least 100,000 people. The organizers rented a 600-acre farm in Bethel and waited for the crowds and performers to show up.

Thousands of young people appeared the day before the concert was scheduled, many of them arriving in the official car of the hippie generation, flower-painted Volkswagen vans. More than 25,000 people had assembled the night before, and they kept coming. By Friday, August 15, most of the roadways surrounding the area were closed due to uncontrollable traffic. Thousands of concertgoers pulled over to the side of the road and walked the final miles. By Saturday, the height of the event, there were about 450,000 young people crowding the farm and the town of Bethel, which had a population of 3,900. The festival could have turned into a disaster because there was not nearly enough food and facilities for the numbers of people. There was no security present, little medical staff, and heavy rain turned the grounds into acres of mud.

The generation that had long proclaimed its belief in peace, love, and understanding, however, lived up to its ideals. Young people listened to their music, shared the supplies they brought (including their drugs), played in the mud, and waited patiently for food and water to be delivered from the outside. There were three deaths, one by drug overdose, one burst appendix, and one by a tractor accident, but there was no reported violence throughout the four days. There were also two births recorded at the concert. The local police chief, a veteran of 24 years, said, "It was the most courteous, considerate, and well-behaved group of kids that I have ever been in contact with."

It was the defining moment for the generation that came of age in the 1960s, a generation that would now be known as the Woodstock Generation. As the decade ended, most of the issues it cared about and protested against, particularly the Vietnam War, remained. Their campaign to change the United States continued into the 1970s.

SPORTS IN THE 1960S

The 1960s were a time of expansion and big television contracts for professional sports. Pro football expanded from 12 to 26 as a new league, the American Football

In December 1969, the Rolling Stones held a free music festival at Altamont Racetrack near San Francisco. The festival was poorly planned, and the notorious motorcycle gang the Hell's Angels was in charge of security. Violence marred the event, resulting in four deaths.

On February 5, 1969, the Federal Communications Commission (FCC) proposed banning cigarette advertising on television and radio. This legislation went into effect in 1971.

COMPUTERS COME ON STAGE

In 1958, U.S. engineer Jack Kilby invented the integrated circuit, the forerunner of the computer microchip, a combination of transistors and other electronic parts. The invention was a breakthrough because chips are capable of performing complex tasks quickly. This invention was the beginning of the modern computer industry. Throughout the 1960s, improvements were made on microchip technology, especially to support NASA and the space program.

In 1963, Digital Equipment Corporation introduced the first minicomputer. Other companies conducted private research to apply the technology to their own needs. In 1965, Bell Telephone developed an electronic switching system to speed up service and prevent system overloads. In 1968, the development of the silicon chip changed the computer industry forever by miniaturizing integrated circuits. This technology enabled many more parts to be designed into a single computer system.

By 1971, three engineers from Intel Corporation had built the first commercial microprocessor, in which each microchip contained thousands of transistors. This event marked the beginning of the computer revolution. Since that time the technology has continued to develop, and microprocessors of the 21st century now contain millions of transistors.

Melba Roy was known as one of NASA's so-called computers. With the help of real computers, she tracks the orbit of the *Echo* satellite. *(NASA)*

League (AFL), was formed in 1960 to compete for players and attendance with the old National Football League (NFL). Baseball expanded for the first time in 60 years, increasing the number of teams from 16 to 24 and doubling its attendance. Professional basketball increased from 8 to 19 teams as the new American Basketball Association (ABA) was formed in 1968 to rival the National Basketball Association (NBA). As the television audience increased in all these new markets, the networks signed million dollar contracts with the leagues. As a result, athletes' salaries soared.

It was football that benefited the most from its television contracts as it became the number one U.S. spectator sport, surpassing even baseball. The competition between the AFL and NFL was a part of this rise, as was the two leagues' organization of the Super Bowl in 1967. This game between the two league champions drew a huge audience, and eventually led to a merger of the two leagues in 1970.

There were also three football legends from the 1960s that helped make football number one U.S. sport. Vince Lombardi was the brilliant coach of the Green Bay Packers, the powerhouse dynasty team of the 1960s. Lombardi used innovative plays and demanding leadership to win five championships during the decade, including the first two Super Bowls. Jim Brown of the Cleveland Browns is often regarded as the greatest running back in the history of the NFL. His combination of speed and strength made him the league's rushing leader in eight of the nine years he played. When he retired at the age of 30 to pursue a movie career, Brown held the league records for rushing yards at 12,312 and touchdowns at 126. Quarterback Johnny Unitas of the Baltimore Colts, another football star of the 1960s, became a football legend in the 1958 title game between the Colts and the New York Giants. He led the Colts to a thrilling 23–17 overtime win that gained nationwide attention for the sport. Over his career, which ended in 1972, he set numerous passing records and led the Colts to three championships, including one Super Bowl in 1971.

Baseball saw a cherished record broken in 1961 when Roger Maris of the New York Yankees hit 61 home runs, surpassing Babe Ruth's record of 60. The baseball heroes of the early 1960s, however, were still Mickey Mantle of the Yankees and Willie Mays of the San Francisco Giants. Both burst onto the scene in the 1950s, starting a debate that lasted their entire careers: who was the best baseball player? Mays had the better statistics, but Mantle won the World Series seven times with the powerful Yankees. In the late 1960s, pitching dominated baseball, and Sandy Koufax of the Los Angeles Dodgers was the game's best player, leading the Dodgers to two World Series victories.

Basketball in the 1960s was dominated by the remarkable dynasty of the Boston Celtics who won the championship nine out of 10 years. The Celtics were led by center Bill Russell, who revolutionized the game by emphasizing rebounding and defense over scoring. He had many legendary battles over the decade with the game's scoring machine, Wilt Chamberlain. Chamberlain once averaged over 50 points a game for

A future Hall of Fame member, Willie Mays was among the biggest stars of the 1960s. *(Library of Congress)*

"Ballplayers don't read the sports pages anymore; they read the Wall Street Journal.*"*

—New York Yankees' pitcher Whitey Ford on the newfound wealth of baseball players in the 1960s

As a member of the Philadelphia Warriors in 1962, Wilt Chamberlain scored 100 points in one game, an NBA record that still stands.

"Float like a butterfly, sting like a bee, his hands can't hit what his eyes can't see."

—Heavyweight boxing champion Muhammad Ali, describing his technique and speed as a fighter

the season, but he could only beat Russell and the Celtics once during the decade, winning the championship in 1967 for the Philadelphia 76ers.

Politics in the Olympics

Sports stayed relatively free of political controversy during the turbulent 1960s with a couple of exceptions. The first was the controversial and popular heavyweight boxing champion Muhammad Ali. Ali won the title in 1964 when he was known as Cassius Clay. After the fight, however, he converted to Islam and assumed his new name. In 1967, Ali refused to be inducted into the U.S. Army on religious grounds and as a protest against the Vietnam War. During the three-year legal battle that ensued, Ali was stripped of his heavyweight title and banned from boxing in the United States. In 1971, the Supreme Court overturned Ali's conviction on draft evasion charges and Ali returned to the ring, eventually regaining his heavyweight title.

Another political incident occurred during the 1968 Summer Olympics in Mexico City. After African-American runners Tommie Smith and John Carlos won the gold and bronze medals for the United States in the 200-meter race, they made a symbolic statement against U.S. racism at the medals ceremony. They wore black socks to represent black poverty and a black glove to represent black power. When the national anthem was played, they lowered their heads and raised their fist in the Black Power salute, a gesture of protest against racism. The Olympics, which strives to keep politics out of the competition, expelled Smith and Carlos from the rest of the games.

THE LEGACY OF THE 1960S

The mood of the 1960s would endure into the early 1970s as America's involvement in the Vietnam War

THE YEAR OF THE UNDERDOG

Two of the biggest upsets in sports history took place in the 1960s, both in 1969. In baseball, the New York Mets had been the laughingstock of the major leagues since it joined the National League in 1962. In its first year, the team lost a record 120 games. In its first seven years, it always finished last or next to last, and it lost over 100 games five times. Entering the 1969 season, the Mets were 100–1 underdogs to win the World Series.

An improbable 1969 season saw the Mets's pitching and brilliant manager, Gil Hodges, lead them to the National League pennant and an appearance in the World Series against the powerful American League champions, the Baltimore Orioles. The Orioles had won 109 games during the season, the most since the 1954 Cleveland Indians, and they were heavy favorites to easily beat the young, inexperienced Mets. The Orioles won the first game, but the Mets swept the next four for the biggest World Series upset in the history of baseball. New York City celebrated by holding the biggest ticker tape parade since V-J day in August 1945, which celebrated the U.S. victory over Japan in World War II.

In football, the New York Jets had the flashiest quarterback, Joe Namath, and won the AFL championship with a narrow victory over the Oakland Raiders. The win gave the Jets a berth in Super Bowl III against the NFL champion, the Baltimore Colts, on January 12, 1969. The AFL was still thought of as the weaker league, and the NFL had proven it with two easy wins by Vince Lombardi's Green Bay Packers in the first two Super Bowls. Namath's Jets were 17-point underdogs, but the brash quarterback guaranteed a Jets victory in Super Bowl III. Namath lived up to his promise and led the Jets to a 16–7 win over the Colts, the biggest upset in Super Bowl history.

---

continued until 1973. The protests would continue also. Most decades have changed American society in some ways, but the 1960s transformed America. Television news coverage made more and more Americans aware of important issues, like civil rights and pollution, which could no longer be ignored. Young people with new ideas dreamed of a better, more peaceful America. Their movement instead created a split in American society, usually labeled liberal vs. conservative, which persists to this day.

The technology boom stimulated by the 1960s space program, especially the advent of the computer, changed daily life forever around the world. One of the results of that space program was a simple, beautiful image of Earth taken from space. The image made many Americans in the 1960s ask themselves how can there be so much conflict when it is clear that humans all share the same home, Earth? It's a question Americans and the rest of the world would continue to struggle with in the decades that followed.

"Winning isn't everything, It's the only thing."

—Green Bay Packers' head coach Vince Lombardi on his coaching philosophy

GLOSSARY

alienation A state of being separate or isolated from one's family or society, especially common among teens.

armory A military building for personnel or storage.

ballistic missile A guided missile that is often carries nuclear weapons and travels long distances to land on a specific target.

beatnik A member of the 1950s counter-culture that rejected the materialism, suburban culture, and cold war mentality of U.S. society.

bouffant hairdo A hair style in which the hair is puffed out in a large, rounded shape.

Buddhism One of the main religions of Asia, based on the teachings of Siddhartha Gautama (ca. 563 B.C.–ca. 483 B.C.) who later became known as the Buddha, or the Enlightened One.

civil disobedience The refusal to obey laws as a form of political protest.

cold war The state of tension, hostility, and limited armed conflicts that developed between capitalist and communist countries after World War II. The main conflict was between the United States and the Soviet Union.

commune A group of people who live together and share possessions,

responsibilities, and a common outlook or philosophy.

communism A system of government in which the state controls all the means of production and establishes a social order in which all goods are shared equally.

conscription Mandatory enrollment for military service; usually called the draft.

contraceptive A device or drug used to prevent pregnancy.

counterculture A culture that rejects the values of the established culture.

coup An overthrow of a government.

disarmament The elimination of a nation's military weapons.

establishment A term used to refer to people and institutions that are part of traditional, mainstream society.

ghetto A city slum populated by a minority group.

guru An influential teacher or popular expert in a cultural movement.

hallucinations Sensory experiences that appear real but are not; sometimes caused by the use of certain drugs, such as LSD.

integration The end of segregation in which people of different races or ethnic groups mingle freely.

microchip A tiny panel of semiconducting material used to make an integrated circuit capable of complex electrical tasks.

microprocessor A microchip that functions as the central processing unit (CPU) of a microcomputer.

mystique A body of beliefs, ideas, and attitudes associated with a particular subject.

nationalists People in favor of political independence for their country or culture.

paisley Design of colorful patterns with curved shapes.

psychedelic Having intense, colorful, and abstract patterns.

satellite A small celestial body or human-made object that orbits a larger celestial body, moon, or planet.

segregation The separation of groups by race or other differences.

self-determination Freedom to choose a course of action or political status without outside interference.

shantytown An area of temporary, rundown shelters.

sitcom A humorous television show; a shortened term for situation comedy.

sit-in A protest in which demonstrators occupy a public place.

Sputnik The first satellites launched into space by Russia during the late 1950s.

suburb A residential area outside a large city.

surveillance Close, secret observation of a suspected enemy.

tie-dying A process in which a piece of fabric or clothing item is knotted up and dipped in several dyes to create splotches of color.

tsunami A tidal wave caused by an earthquake.

vendetta A prolonged campaign of hostile acts to destroy a person's reputation.

Vietnamization President Nixon's plan to slowly withdraw U.S. troops from Vietnam and give the South Vietnamese army the responsibility to fight the war.

wiretap A device that makes it possible for an outsider to secretly listen to others' private conversations.

FURTHER READING

BOOKS

Andrew, John A. *Lyndon Johnson and the Great Society*. Chicago: I. R. Dee, 1998.

Bond, Peter. *Reaching for the Stars: The Illustrated History of Manned Spaceflight*. London: Cassell, 1993.

Bromell, Nick. *Tomorrow Never Knows: Rock and Psychedelics in the 1960s*. Chicago: University of Chicago Press, 2002.

Burner, David. *Making Peace with the 60s*. Princeton, N.J.: Princeton University Press, 1996.

Burns, Stewart. *Social Movements of the 1960s: Searching for Democracy*. Boston: Twayne, 1990.

Carson, Rachel. *Silent Spring*. Boston: Houghton Mifflin, 2002.

Colbert, Nancy A. *Great Society: The Story of Lyndon Baines Johnson*. Greensboro, N.C.: Morgan Reynolds, 2002.

Connikie, Yvonne. *Fashions of a Decade: The 1960s*. New York: Facts On File, 1991.

Davis, Flora. *Moving the Mountain: The Women's Movement in America since 1960*. New York: Simon & Schuster, 1991.

Divine, Robert A. *The Sputnik Challenge*. New York: Oxford, 1993.

Epstein, Dan. *Twentieth-Century Pop Culture: The 60s*. Philadelphia: Chelsea House, 2001.

Farmer, James, and Don E. Carleton. *Lay Bare the Heart: An Autobiography of the Civil Rights Movement*. Fort Worth, Tex.: Texas Christian University, 1998.

Feinstein, Stephen. *The 1960s: From the Vietnam War to Flower Power*. Berkeley Heights, N.J.: Enslow, 2000.

Fries, Chuck, and Wilson, Irv. *We'll Never Be Young Again*. Los Angeles: Tallfellow Press, 2003.

Gitlin, Todd. *The Sixties: Years of Hope, Days of Rage*. New York: Bantam, 1993.

Gould, Lewis. *1968: The Election That Changed America*. Chicago: I. R. Dee, 1993.

Graham, Hugh Davis. *Civil Rights and the Presidency*. New York: Oxford, 1992.

Hall, Mitchell K. *The Vietnam War*. New York: Longman, 2000.

Harrington, Michael. *The Other America*. New York: Scribner, 1997.

Hoffman, Elizabeth Cobbs. *All You Need Is Love: The Peace Corps and the Spirit of the 1960s*. Cambridge, Mass.: Harvard University Press, 1998.

Holland, Gina. *The 1960s: A Cultural History of the United States*. San Diego: Lucent, 1999.

Hunt, Michael. *Lyndon Johnson's War: America's Cold War Crusade in Vietnam, 1945–1968*. New York: Hill & Wang, 1997.

Isserman, Maurice, and Michael Kazin. *America Divided: The Civil War of the 1960s*. New York: Oxford, 2000.

Kaiser, Michael. *1968 in America: Music, Politics, Chaos, Counterculture and the Shaping of a Generation*. New York: Grove Press, 1997.

Kennedy, John F. *Profiles in Courage*. New York: Perennial, 2000.

Kleinfelder, Rita Lang. *When We Were Young: A Baby-Boomer Yearbook*. New York: Prentice Hall, 1993.

Kronenwetter, Michael. *America in the 1960s*. San Diego: Lucent, 1998.

Landy, Elliott. *Woodstock Vision: The Spirit of a Generation*. New York: Continuum Publishing, 1994.

Law, Lisa, and Ram Dass. *Flashing on the Sixties*. Santa Rosa, Calif.: Squarebooks, 2000.

Maga, Timothy. *The 1960s: An Eyewitness History*. New York: Facts On File, 2003.

Margolis, Jon. *The Last Innocent Year: America in 1964: The Beginning of the "Sixties."* New York: Morrow, 1999.

Marty, Myron A. *Daily Life in the United States, 1960–1990: Decades of Discord*. Westport, Conn.: Greenwood, 1997.

McAdam, Doug. *Freedom Summer*. New York: Oxford, 1990.

McWilliams, John C. *The 1960s Cultural Revolution*. Westport, Conn.: Greenwood, 2000.

Morgan, Edward P. *The 60s Experience: Hard Lessons about Modern America*. Philadelphia: Temple University Press, 1991.

Morrison, Joan. *From Camelot to Kent State: The Sixties Experience in the Words of Those Who Lived It*. New York: Oxford, 1987.

Murray, Charles, and Catherine Bly Cox. *Apollo: The Race for the Moon*. New York: Touchstone, 1990.

O'Neil, Doris C., ed. *Life: The 60s*. New York: Bulfinch, 1991.

Pichaske, David R. *A Generation in Motion: Popular Music and Culture in the Sixties*. Boston: Ellis, 1989.

Posner, Gerald. *Killing the Dream: James Earl Ray and the Assassination of Martin Luther King*. New York: Random House, 1998

Rielly, Edward J. *The 1960s: American Popular Culture Through History*. Westport, Conn.: Greenwood, 2003.

Rubel, David. *The United States in the 20th Century*. New York: Scholastic, 1995.

Singleton, Carl, ed. *The Sixties in America* (3 vols.), Pasadena, Calif: Salem, 1999.

Stern, Jane, and Michael Stern. *Sixties People*. New York: Knopf, 1990.

Stern, Mark. *Calculating Visions: Kennedy, Johnson, and Civil Rights*. New Brunswick, N.J.: Rutgers University Press, 1992.

Time-Life Editors. *Turbulent Years: The 1960s*. Alexandria, Va.: Time-Life Books, 1998.

White, Mark J. *Missiles in Cuba: Kennedy, Khrushchev, Castro, and the 1962 Crisis*. Chicago: I. R. Dee, 1998.

White, Mark J., ed. *Kennedy: The New Frontier Revisited*. New York: New York University Press, 1998.

Williams, Juan. *Eyes on the Prize: America's Civil Rights Years, 1954–1965*. New York: Viking, 1987.

Witcover, Jules. *The Year the Dream Died: Revisiting 1968 in America*. New York: Warner Books, 1997.

Wofford, Harris. *Of Kennedys and Kings: Making Sense of the Sixties*. Pittsburgh, Penn.: University of Pittsburgh Press, 1992.

WEBSITES

Kingwood College Library. "American Cultural History: the Twentieth Century." Available online. URL: http://kclibrary.nhmccd.edu/decade60.html. Downloaded in July 2005.

National Parks Department. "We Shall Overcome: Historic Places of the Civil Rights Movement." Available online. URL: http://www.cr.nps.gov/nr/travel/civilrights Downloaded in July 2005.

New York University Archives. 1968 revisited. Available online. URL: http://www.nyu.edu/library/bobst/collections/exhibits/arch/Homepg/Index.html. Downloaded in July 2005.

PBS. "Battlefield: Vietnam." Available online. URL: http://www.pbs.org/battlefieldvietnam. Downloaded in July 2005.

University of Minnesota—Twin Cities. "U.S. History: Internet Resources, the 1960s." URL http://www.hist.umn.edu/~hist20c/internet/1960s.htm. Downloaded in July 2005.

INDEX

Page numbers in *italics* indicate illustrations. Page numbers followed by *g* indicate glossary entries. Page numbers in **boldface** indicate box features.